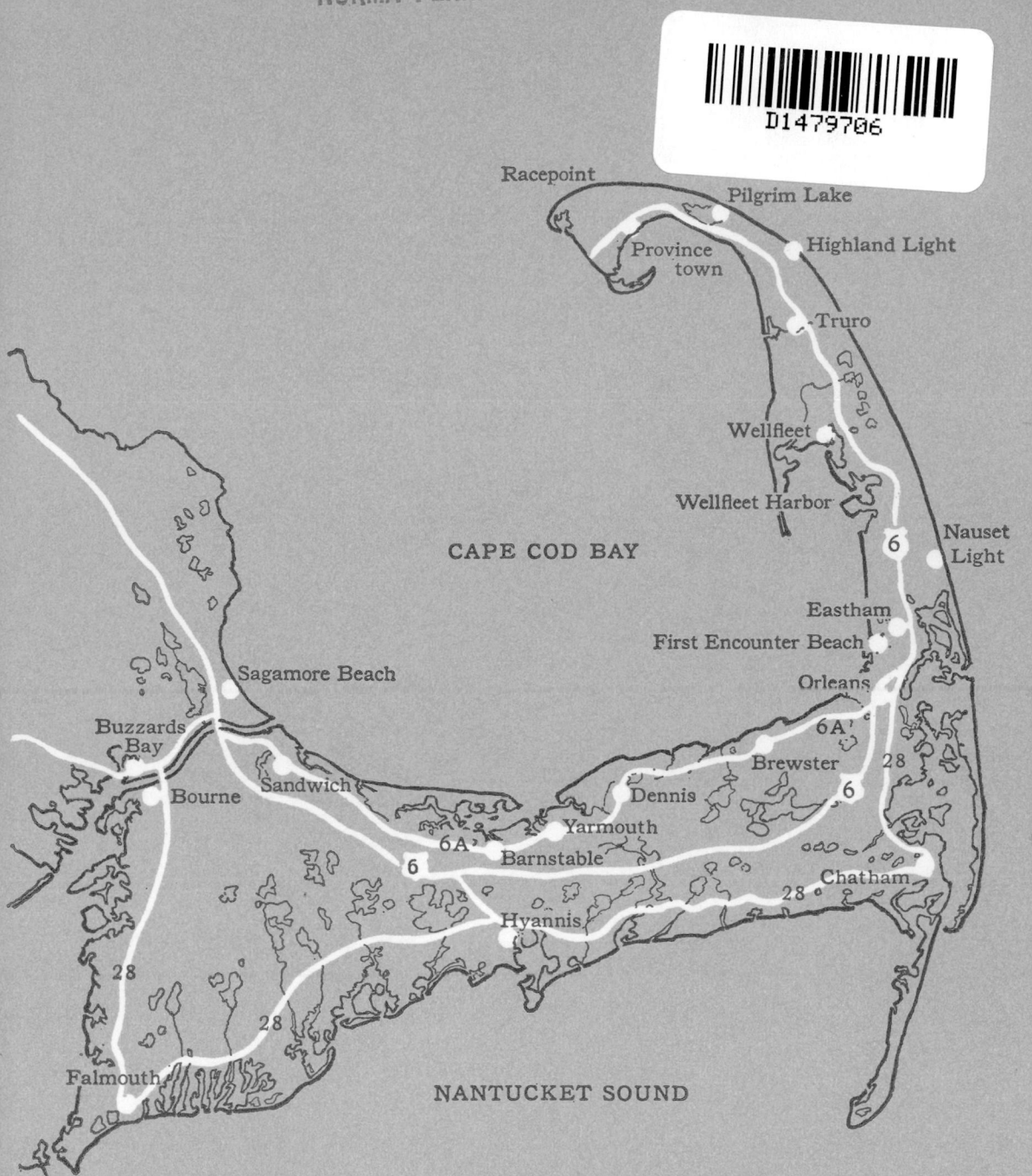

Racepoint

Pilgrim Lake

Highland Light

Province town

Truro

Wellfleet

Wellfleet Harbor

Nauset Light

CAPE COD BAY

6

Eastham

First Encounter Beach

Sagamore Beach

Orleans

6A

Buzzards Bay

Brewster

28

Bourne

Sandwich

Dennis

6

Yarmouth

6

6A

Barnstable

Chatham

28

Hyannis

28

28

Falmouth

NANTUCKET SOUND

THOREAU'S GUIDE TO *Cape Cod*

Thoreau's Guide to

(Based on *Cape Cod* by Henry David Thoreau)

Edited and illustrated by **Alexander B. Adams**

With a biographical sketch of

Thoreau by Ralph Waldo Emerson

The Devin-Adair Company ❦ New York

CAPE

COD

to CLANCY *and* LOUISE HORTON
who are also good guides to Cape Cod

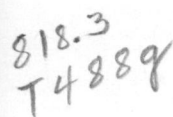

Contents

A Note to the Reader

Cape Cod is a wind-lashed, sandy point that extends for almost thirty-five miles due east from the Massachusetts coast into the Atlantic and then turns abruptly north for another thirty. It ends at the fishing village of Provincetown in a mass of dunes and shoals that tumble into the ocean's rim, but exactly where it starts is more difficult to determine.

Speak to a man at Wareham or Onset on the eastern shore of Buzzards Bay and, particularly if he has an interest in cranberries or the tourist trade, he will claim to be part of the Cape and the Cape tradition, a claim that will be warmly denied by the residents of Osterville or Wianno, which lie on the point itself. Yet mention Osterville or Wianno in turn to a sea captain living in greater isolation at Wellfleet, and he is likely to dismiss both towns with the curt comment, "Summer people."

To settle the issue, the practical-minded may suggest placing the boundary at the ship canal, which cuts through the narrow neck of land that divides Buzzards Bay from Cape Cod Bay. But as a boundary marker even the Canal has severe limitations, because it includes such distinctly non-Cape Cod areas as Camp Edwards and the Otis Air Base.

At the root of the problem of defining Cape Cod is the basic fact that the Cape is not so much a piece of geography as a state of mind and an attitude toward life, so that each individual must interpret it in his own way. Consequently, for some, Cape Cod begins at the threshold of a centuries-old house whose silver-gray shingles have never known the touch of paint; for others, at the first sight of the waves pounding against the long reaches of the Outer Beach or of clammers working the flats at low tide. In every case, the decision is, and must be, a personal one.

Like its geography, Cape Cod's history too is largely a matter of individual taste. The Cape has a small quota of formal events, as must any place in the New World discovered as early as 1602. For example, the first recorded death of a European by violence in New England occurred at Nauset Harbor. In 1620 the Pilgrims sighted Cape Cod, stopped for almost two months in Provincetown Harbor, made several exploratory trips, and then went on to Plymouth. Another important occasion in the Cape's history was the opening of the Canal in 1914. It cut seventy miles from the voyage between New York and Boston and made heavy inroads into two historic Cape industries: rescuing shipwrecked sailors and searching the shores for salvage, called wrecking. But for the most part, the Cape's history is composed of smaller, local incidents, each with its own color and interest, yet hardly the sort that can be followed from point to point with the help of numbers on a map.

Obviously, to provide a guidebook to such a region takes a writer of unusual talent, one with sensitivity and insight, who can enlarge the traveler's understanding but accomplish this with few facts, figures or dates. Such a writer was Henry David Thoreau, who, with two objectives in mind, made the first of several trips to Cape Cod in 1849. Already familiar with the woods and fields of New England, he now wanted to acquaint himself with its ocean, and hoped at the same time to gather material for at least one magazine article. Setting out with his friend Ellery Channing, he used public transportation as far as Orleans, which is roughly the start of the Lower Cape, or the point where it turns north, and proceeded the rest of the way on foot. He made other trips in 1855 and 1857.

The first hundred pages of Thoreau's manuscript went off to the editor of *Putnam's Monthly* at the end of 1852, but the work did not start appearing serially until 1855; and then Thoreau suddenly withdrew it because of a controversy with the editor. In 1865, some three years after Thoreau's death, it was finally published in book form.[1]

In several respects, *Cape Cod* was an act of journalism rather than an act of art. Thoreau was writing for a relatively wide audience, and he also hoped to get paid for the article by the page. As a result he rambled in many places, indulged in what one critic calls "journalistic jocosity," and included many inconsequential quotations from local historians and other writers. About the latter even Thoreau himself had some misgivings; he wrote the editor that he was "in doubt about the extracts from the old ministers," and gave permission either to delete them or to run them in smaller type, a considerable concession from a man who would sometimes fight over changing a single sentence.

But because Thoreau had the attributes of genius and because he and his subject were ideally suited to each other, his book also contains some of the best material ever written about the Cape, material that is as alive and pertinent today as when Thoreau first wrote it. For example, he committed to paper as no one else has the wind whistling over the scrub pines and the sound of waves breaking against the shore, and one who has read his description of the Atlantic can never look at that ocean again without thinking of what Thoreau said. His work is essential to a real understanding of the Cape and what it means.

The purpose of this volume is not to provide another edition of *Cape Cod* but to emphasize the best in that book and also rearrange it so it forms an up-to-date guidebook which today's traveler can use. Consequently, two criteria governed the selection of each passage: was it one of those in which Thoreau set

[1 The edition from which all excerpts in this book are taken is that of W. W. Norton & Company, New York, published in 1951.]

aside the digressions that sometimes tempted him and truly captured the spirit of the Cape, and was it descriptive, at least for the most part, of a sight that a visitor can see today? The paragraphs that met these standards were then arranged under topical headings so that the traveling reader can quickly find Thoreau's comments on any particular subject. As a further convenience, the material was also placed in rough geographical sequence, moving from south to north. At the start of each section appear additional comments that may help today's visitor find his way and also serve to amplify Thoreau's remarks.

While an organized tour of the Cape is to be avoided as a spiritual heresy—Cape Cod does not lend itself to organization—the reader will find that this book develops logically, if he starts at the town of Eastham, which can be easily reached by taking Route 6. Eastham lies at the edge of the Cape Cod National Seashore. At Eastham, the reader can take a look at the town, visit the old windmill which still stands there, and then proceed northeast to the Nauset Lights. From there he can move north, keeping as Thoreau did partly to the shore and partly inland, being sure, of course, to visit the old town of Wellfleet. Then he can go on to Truro, the Highland Light, the Clay Pounds, up through the "wrist" of the Cape, past the giant sand dunes and on into Provincetown. At Provincetown he can explore Race Point and the other outlying areas and end his trip there, as Thoreau did.

By following this general procedure, the sights he reads about in this book will unfold around him. He will then be traveling through that state of mind and attitude toward life that is called Cape Cod, and his personal guide will be one of America's greatest writers, Henry David Thoreau.

Alexander B. Adams

Westport, Connecticut

THOREAU'S GUIDE TO *Cape Cod*

ACKNOWLEDGMENTS

No book is created by one person alone. In this instance, four individuals, who—for understandable reasons of professional modesty—prefer not to be named, shared with me many helpful suggestions and that rare, but important human quality, enthusiasm. The general reader will not recognize them from these remarks, but I hope that they will recognize themselves.

My children, Harriet, George and Elliott, deserve thanks for keeping me company on my photographic trips, taking notes and helping to read the proofs. George also took much responsibility in preparing the index.

And as to the inevitable acknowledgment to my wife? She and I have shared so long and so closely in so many endeavors that to thank her expressly would be almost like thanking a part of myself.

ABOUT THE PHOTOGRAPHS

To see Cape Cod with my camera as another man saw it more than a hundred years ago presented an interesting challenge in the use of photography, because it had to be his eye looking through the view-finder, not mine. To achieve this, I first had to familiarize myself with Thoreau's mental outlook, and so I made several trips to Concord and Walden and, of course, read widely, finding Thoreau's correspondence especially valuable, because it revealed his day-to-day attitudes and thinking.

Next I reviewed the text of *Cape Cod,* studying those passages that lent themselves to visual interpretation. When I took the actual photographs, however, I did not work directly from these passages. To do so, I felt, would have had a restrictive effect. Only after the pictures were completed did I match them against specific quotations from the text, in the course of which I discarded many pictures that appealed to me but which seemed more my own than Thoreau's.

In particular, the question of visual anachronisms was bothersome. Electric wires, automobiles, styles of clothing and boats powered by motors proved to be recurrent problems. I decided to ignore electric wires; our eyes have grown so accustomed to them that we do not truly see them. Automobiles I avoided completely; there was no need to include them. As to clothing styles, I determined to use human figures only when necessary and then in as abstract a form as possible. Boats presented a real difficulty. For what is Cape Cod without boats? I finally photographed them in every conceivable position—lying in cradles, careened on the beach and resting at harbor— in every position, that is, except in motion, when the difference between sail and motor power is most apparent.

Pilgrim Lake, which was once open to the sea, and Highland Light, which has been rebuilt since Thoreau's day, presented specific problems; but I decided that the changes that have occurred were inconsequential to Thoreau's mood.

Because I wanted the photographs to stimulate the reader's imagination and to show him what had once stimulated Thoreau, I purposefully avoided identifying each picture by the place where it was taken. My objective was not to provide an illustrated guide to Thoreau's travels but to present in pictorial fashion what he had felt about the Cape.

A. B. A.

Cape Cod

One Cape Cod town, while admitting that most people use automobiles to get there, boasts in its official literature that it can be reached by almost every type of transportation. But in fact automobiles alone are the only practical way to see the Cape. Though a railroad runs the length of the Cape, the rail service has been poor or nonexistent for years, and bus and plane service is limited. In the summer season, plane reservations should be made months ahead of time, for many of them are taken up by regular commuters. There is also a small shuttle plane that runs between Boston and Provincetown. A motorist can reach the Cape by crossing the Canal at Bourne or at Sagamore. To reach Eastham, where this guide starts, the latter is preferable, because it leads directly to Routes 6 and 6-A; 6-A runs through the interesting old towns on Cape Cod Bay, but Route 6 will prove faster to Eastham. Route 28, which begins at Bourne, will take the traveler along the edge of Buzzards Bay and Nantucket Sound, but it is considerably longer. From Eastham, Route 6 is the only main route for reaching Provincetown at the tip of the Cape.

Cape Cod

Cape Cod is the bared and bended arm of Massachusetts: the shoulder is at Buzzard's Bay; the elbow, or crazy-bone, at Cape Mallebarre; the wrist at Truro; and the sandy fist at Provincetown,—behind which the State stands on her guard, with her back to the Green Mountains, and her feet planted on the floor of the ocean, like an athlete protecting her Bay,— boxing with northeast storms, and, ever and anon, heaving up her Atlantic adversary from the lap of earth,—ready to thrust forward her other fist, which keeps guard the while upon her breast at Cape Ann.

. . . . .

. . . [The Cape] has an average breadth of about five miles. In the interior it rises to the height of two hundred, and sometimes perhaps three hundred feet above the level of the sea. According to Hitchcock, the geologist of the State, it is composed almost entirely of sand, even to the depth of three hundred feet in some places, though there is probably a concealed core of rock a little beneath the surface, and it is of diluvian origin, excepting a small portion at the extremity and elsewhere along the shores, which is alluvial. For the first half of the Cape large blocks of stone are found, here and there, mixed with the sand, but for the last thirty miles boulders, or even gravel, are rarely met with. Hitchcock conjectures that the ocean has, in course of time, eaten out Boston Harbor and other bays in the mainland, and that the minute fragments have been deposited by the currents at a distance from the shore, and formed this sand-bank.[1] Above the sand, if the surface is subjected to agricultural tests, there is found to be a thin layer of soil gradually diminishing from Barnstable to Truro, where it ceases; but there are many holes and rents in this weather-beaten garment not likely to be stitched in time, which reveal the naked flesh of the Cape, and its extremity is completely bare.

[1 Geologists today agree that the glaciers created the Cape.—A.B.A.]

. . . . .

The barren aspect of the land would hardly be believed if described. It was such soil, or rather land, as to judge from appearances, no farmer in the interior would think of cultivating, or even fencing. Generally, the ploughed fields of the Cape look white and yellow, like a mixture of salt and Indian meal. This is called soil. All an inlander's notions of soil and fertility will be confounded by a visit to these parts, and he will not be able, for some time afterward, to distinguish soil from sand. The historian of Chatham says of a part of that town, which has been gained from the sea: "There is a doubtful appearance of a soil beginning to be formed. It is styled *doubtful,* because it would not be observed by every eye, and perhaps not acknowledged by many."

We thought that this would not be a bad description of the greater part of the Cape. There is a "beach" on the west side of Eastham, which we crossed the next summer, half a mile wide, and stretching across the township, containing seventeen hundred acres on which there is not now a particle of vegetable mould, though it formerly produced wheat. All sands are here called "beaches," whether they are waves of water or of air, that dash against them, since they commonly have their origin on the shore.

⋘ Eastham

Eastham was incorporated in 1646 under the name Nauset, which was changed to Eastham in 1651. It originally included such other towns as Wellfleet, Orleans, Brewster, and most of Chatham and Harwich. One of its original settlers was Governor John Prence, who so disliked leaving home that much of the colony's business was conducted at Eastham. In effect, the town became the capital of the Plymouth Colony during his term in office. The visitor would do well to spend some time here before following the rest of Thoreau's trip. By taking Samoset Road, which leads to the left from Route 6, he will come to First Encounter Beach, where the Pilgrims first met the Indians. This part of Cape Cod Bay is so shallow that it is possible to walk many hundreds of yards out from shore at low tide. The incoming tide, however, advances so rapidly that the visitor should exercise some caution. This is a favorite place for clamming, and the ebb and flood of the tides is well worth watching. The ship lying off the shore is used as a target for bombing and rocket practice. Another worthwhile place in Eastham is the Coast Guard Beach, reached by taking the first right after passing the Salt Pond north of the town hall. The Coast Guard station is no longer in operation; but the beach, with the salt bays behind it and the ocean in front, is an excellent spot to feel the whole temper of the Cape. More detailed information about Eastham can be obtained either from the town-operated information center on Route 6 or at the town hall.

 ⚎  The ecclesiastical history of this town interested us somewhat. It appears that "they very early built a small meeting-house, twenty feet square, with a thatched roof through which they might fire their muskets,"—of course, at the Devil. "In 1662, the town agreed that a part of every whale[1] cast on shore be appropriated for the support of the ministry." No doubt there seemed to be some propriety in thus leaving the support of the ministers to Providence, whose servants they are, and who alone rules the storms; for, when few whales were cast up, they might suspect that their worship was not acceptable. The ministers must have sat upon the cliffs in every storm, and watched the shore with anxiety. And, for my part, if I were a minister, I would rather trust to the bowels of the billows, on the back-side of Cape Cod, to cast up a whale for me, than to the generosity of many a country parish that I know. You cannot say of a country minister's salary, commonly, that it is "very like a whale."

Nevertheless, the minister who depended on whales cast up must have had a trying time of it. I would rather have gone to the Falkland Isles with a harpoon, and done with it. Think of a whale having the breath of life beaten out of him by a storm, and dragging in over the bars and guzzles, for the support of the ministry! What a consolation it must have been to him! I have heard of a minister, who had been a fisherman, being settled in Bridgewater for as long a time as he could tell a cod from a haddock. Generous as it seems, this condition would empty most country pulpits forthwith, for it is long since the fishers of men

[1 After an absence of a hundred years, right whales, which were the most important whales to the whaling industry, are beginning to reappear in Cape Cod's waters. Their numbers, of course, are still extremely limited.—A.B.A.]

were fishermen. Also, a duty was put on mackerel here to support a free-school; in other words, the mackerel-school was taxed in order that the children's school might be free.

"In 1665 the Court passed a law to inflict corporal punishment on all persons, who resided in the towns of this government, who denied the Scriptures." Think of a man being whipped on a spring morning, till he was constrained to confess that the Scriptures were true! "It was also voted by the town, that all persons who should stand out of the meeting-house during the time of divine service should be set in the stocks." It behooved such a town to see that sitting in the meeting-house was nothing akin to sitting in the stocks, lest the penalty of obedience to the law might be greater than that of disobedience.

ⵊ Windmills

Just opposite the town hall in Eastham on Route 6 is a windmill that is open to visitors. According to tradition, it was built in Plymouth in 1793, floated across Cape Cod Bay to Provincetown, and then later moved to Eastham. Until the 1880s it was operated by a full-time miller. Today it is owned by the town of Eastham. Windmills such as this one were once widely used on the Cape for grinding grain and for pumping brine for the salt works.

ⵊ   The most foreign and picturesque structures on the Cape, to an inlander, not excepting the salt-works, are the windmills, —gray-looking, octagonal towers, with long timbers slanting to the ground in the rear, and there resting on a cartwheel, by which their fans are turned round to face the wind. These appeared also to serve in some measure for props against its force. A great circular rut was worn around the building by the wheel. The neighbors who assemble to turn the mill to the wind are likely to know which way it blows, without a weather-cock. They looked loose and slightly locomotive, like huge wounded birds, trailing a wing or a leg, and reminded one of pictures of the Netherlands.

9

Being on elevated ground, and high in themselves, they serve as landmarks,—for there are no tall trees, or other objects commonly, which can be seen at a distance in the horizon; though the outline of the land itself is so firm and distinct, that an insignificant cone, or even precipice of sand, is visible at a great distance from over the sea. Sailors making the land commonly steer either by the windmills, or the meeting-houses. In the country, we are obliged to steer by the meeting-houses alone. Yet the meeting-house is a kind of windmill, which runs one day in seven, turned either by the winds of doctrine or public opinion, or more rarely by the winds of Heaven, where another sort of grist is ground, of which, if it be not all bran or musty, if it be not *plaster,* we trust to make bread of life.

⋙ The Houses

The typical Cape Cod cottage is so practical in its design that it has been duplicated throughout the United States. Many fine old examples of the original houses still remain on the Cape, and they are well worth close examination. When ordering a house from the carpenter, the prospective owner stated whether he wanted a full house, a three-quarters house, or a half-house. A full house has four windows on the front, two on each side of the door; a three-quarters house has only three windows, one on one side of the door and two on the other; a half-house has two windows, both on the same side of the door. These changes in exterior design are obvious reflections of the overall sizes of the houses.

⋙ We walked with our umbrellas behind us since it blowed hard as well as rained, with driving mists, as the day before and the wind helped us over the sand at a rapid rate. Everything indicated that we had reached a strange shore. The road was a mere lane, winding over bare swells of bleak and barren-looking land. The houses were few and far between, besides being small and rusty, though they appeared to be kept in good repair, and their door-yards, which were the unfenced Cape, were tidy; or

11

rather, they looked as if the ground around them was blown clean by the wind. Perhaps the scarcity of wood here, and the consequent absence of the wood-pile and other wooden traps, had something to do with this appearance. They seemed, like mariners ashore, to have sat right down to enjoy the firmness of the land, without studying their postures or habiliments. To them it was merely *terra firma* and *cognita,* not yet *fertilis* and *jucunda.*

. . . . .

The great number of windows in the ends of the houses, and their irregularity in size and position, here and elsewhere on the Cape, struck us agreeably,—as if each of the various occupants who had their *cunabula* behind had punched a hole where his necessities required it, and according to his size and stature, without regard to outside effect. There were windows for the grown folks, and windows for the children,—three or four apiece; as a certain man had a large hole cut in his barn-door for the cat, and another smaller one for the kitten. Sometimes they were so low under the eaves that I thought they must have perforated the plate beam for another apartment, and I noticed some which were triangular, to fit that part more exactly. The ends of the houses had thus as many muzzles as a revolver, and, if the inhabitants have the same habit of staring out the windows that some of our neighbors have, a traveler must stand a small chance with them.

Generally, the old-fashioned and unpainted houses on the Cape looked more comfortable, as well as picturesque, than the modern and more pretending ones, which were less in harmony with the scenery, and less firmly planted. These houses were on the shores of a chain of ponds, seven in number, the source of a small stream called Herring River, which empties into the Bay. There are many Herring Rivers on the Cape; they will, perhaps, be more numerous than herrings soon.

The Plains of Nauset

The Nauset Indian tribe, after whom this area to the north of Eastham is named, once occupied the whole of this part of the Cape, and were among those who owed allegiance to Chief Massasoit and later to his son, King Philip. In 1615 several of their number were kidnapped by Thomas Hunt, one of Captain John Smith's men. Hunt sold his captives as slaves in Spain. In spite of this act, the Nausets were later to prove themselves good friends of the Pilgrims on many occasions, bringing them news of approaching ships, selling them corn, and several times helping rescue lost persons. One obstacle to good relations between the whites and the Indians, however, was Captain Myles Standish, the Pilgrims' military commander. More of a soldier than a diplomat, he constantly regarded the Indians with suspicion.

. . . We found ourselves at once on an apparently boundless plain, without a tree or a fence, or, with one or two exceptions, a house in sight. Instead of fences, the earth was sometimes thrown up into a slight ridge. My companion compared it to the rolling prairies of Illinois. In the storm of wind and rain which raged when we traversed it, it no doubt appeared more vast and

13

desolate than it really is. As there were no hills, but only here and there a dry hollow in the midst of the waste, and the distant horizon was concealed by mist, we did not know whether it was high or low.

A solitary traveler, whom we saw perambulating in the distance, loomed like a giant. He appeared to walk slouchingly, as if held up from above by straps under his shoulders, as much as supported by the plain below. Men and boys would have appeared alike at a little distance, there being no object by which to measure them. Indeed, to an inlander, the Cape landscape is a constant mirage. This kind of country extended a mile or two each way. These were the "Plains of Nauset," once covered with wood, where in winter the winds howl and the snow blows right merrily in the face of the traveler.

⬠ The Ancient Ocean

As Thoreau suggests, the ocean is one of the great sights that the Cape has to offer, but it cannot be appreciated in haste. Not only does it vary in appearance and behavior from hour to hour, but at the same moment, it may be acting differently at different places along the shore. At Race Point, for example, it may appear relatively still and quiet while at Eastham enormous breakers are rolling up on the beaches. To go swimming on a rough day is to feel firsthand the power of the ocean, an experience that every Cape visitor should undergo. However, a word of caution: the waves are often strong enough to toss a 250-pound man, and sometimes an undertow develops that can pull even a strong swimmer farther out to sea than he may want to go. Ordinary safety precautions should always be observed.

⬠ All the morning we had heard the sea roar on the eastern shore, which was several miles distant; . . . though a schoolboy, whom we overtook, hardly knew what we meant, his ears were so used to it. He would have more plainly heard the same sound in a shell. It was a very inspiriting sound to walk by, filling the whole air, that of the sea dashing against the land, heard several miles inland. Instead of having a dog to growl before your door, to have an Atlantic Ocean to growl for a whole Cape! On the whole, we were glad of the storm, which would show us the ocean in its angriest mood. Charles Darwin was assured that the roar of the surf on the coast of Chiloe, after a heavy gale, could be heard at night a distance of "21 sea miles across a hilly and wooded country."

· · · · ·

At length we reached the seemingly retreating boundary of the plain, and entered what had appeared at a distance an up-land marsh, but proved to be dry sand covered with beach-grass, the bearberry,[1] bayberry, shrub-oaks, and beach-plum,[2] slightly ascending as we approached the shore; then, crossing over a belt of sand on which nothing grew, though the roar of the sea sounded scarcely louder than before, and we were prepared to go half a mile farther, we suddenly stood on the edge of a bluff overlooking the Atlantic.

Far below us was the beach, from half a dozen to a dozen rods in width, with a long line of breakers rushing to the strand. The sea was exceedingly dark and stormy, the sky completely over-cast, the clouds still dropping rain, and the wind seemed to blow not so much as the exciting cause, as from sympathy with the already agitated ocean. The waves broke on the bars at some dis-tance from the shore, and curving green or yellow as if over so many unseen dams, ten or twelve feet high, like a thousand waterfalls, rolled in foam to the sand. There was nothing but that savage ocean between us and Europe.

· · · · ·

The white breakers were rushing to the shore; the foam ran up the sand, and then ran back as far as we could see—and we

[1 Bearberry (*Arctostaphylos uva-ursi*), a member of the heath family, is a trailing hillside plant that grows in dry soil.—A.B.A.]
[2 Beach-plums (*Prunus maritima*) are a familiar part of the Cape Codder's diet, being used to make jelly. Many roadside stands still offer this jelly for sale to visitors, and it is well worth stopping for.—A.B.A.]

16

imagined how much farther along the Atlantic coast, before and behind us—as regularly, to compare great things with small, as the master of a choir beats time with his white wand; and ever and anon a higher wave caused us hastily to deviate from our path, and we looked back on our tracks filled with water and foam. The breakers looked like droves of a thousand wild horses of Neptune, rushing to the shore, with their white manes streaming far behind; and when, at length, the sun shone for a moment, their manes were rainbowtinted. Also, the long kelpweed was tossed up from time to time, like the tails of sea-cows sporting in the brine.

. . . . .

The ocean is but a larger lake. At midsummer you may sometimes see a strip of glassy smoothness on it, a few rods in width and many miles long, as if the surface there were covered with a thin pellicle of oil, just as on a country pond; a sort of standstill, you would say, at the meeting or parting of two currents of air—if it does not rather mark the unrippled steadiness of a current of water beneath—for sailors tell of the ocean and land breeze meeting between the fore and aft sails of a vessel, while the latter are full, the former being suddenly taken aback.

. . . . .

Yet this same placid Ocean, as civil now as a city's harbor, a place for ships and commerce, will erelong be lashed into sudden fury, and all its caves and cliffs will resound with tumult. It will ruthlessly heave these vessels to and fro, break them in pieces in its sandy or stony jaws, and deliver their crews to sea-monsters. It will play with them like seaweed, distend them like dead frogs, and carry them about, now high, now low, to show to the fishes, giving them a nibble. This gentle Ocean will toss and tear the rag of a man's body like the father of mad bulls, and his relatives may be seen seeking the remnants for weeks along the strand. From some quiet inland hamlet they have rushed weeping to the unheard-of shore, and now stand uncertain where a sailor has recently been buried amid the sand-hills.

. . . . .

. . . We do not associate the idea of antiquity with the ocean, nor wonder how it looked a thousand years ago, as we do of the land, for it was equally wild and unfathomable always. The Indians have left no traces on its surface, but it is the same to the civilized man and the savage. The aspect of the shore only has changed. The ocean is a wilderness reaching round the globe, wilder than a Bengal jungle, and fuller of monsters, washing the very wharves of our cities and the gardens of our seaside residences. Serpents, bears, hyenas, tigers, rapidly vanish as civilization advances, but the most populous and civilized city cannot scare a shark far from its wharves. It is no further advanced than Singapore, with its tigers, in this respect.

. . . . .

The seashore is a sort of neutral ground, a most advantageous point from which to contemplate this world. It is even a trivial place. The waves forever rolling to the land are too far-traveled and untamable to be familiar. Creeping along the endless beach amid the sun-squall and the foam, it occurs to us that we, too, are the product of sea-slime.

It is a wild, rank place, and there is no flattery in it. Strewn with crabs, horse-shoes, and razor-clams, and whatever the sea casts up,—a vast *morgue,* where famished dogs may range in packs, and crows come daily to glean the pittance which the tide leaves them. The carcasses of men and beasts together lie stately up upon its shelf, rotting and bleaching in the sun and waves, and each tide turns them in their beds, and tucks fresh sand under them. There is naked Nature,—inhumanly sincere, wasting no thought on man, nibbling at the cliffy shore where gulls wheel amid the spray.

From the Nauset Lights

One of the problems of the early lighthouse builders was making each light distinguishable from any others that might be nearby. At Nauset this problem was solved by constructing three lights. One of these still remains, standing to the right of the visitor as he looks out to the ocean from the end of Cable Road. The light on his left is a later one. If he keeps a sharp lookout on his right as he returns down Cable Road, he will see a private house constructed out of the other two Nauset Lights. They were purchased from the federal government and moved back from the shore.

For sixteen miles, commencing at the Nauset Lights, the bank held its height, though farther north it was not so level as here, but interrupted by slight hollows, and the patches of beach-grass and bayberry frequently crept into the sand to its edge. There are some pages entitled "A Description of the Eastern Coast of the County of Barnstable," printed in 1802, pointing out the spots on which the Trustees of the Humane Society have erected huts called Charity or Humane Houses, "and other places where shipwrecked seamen may look for shelter." Two thousand copies of this were dispersed, that every vessel which frequented this coast might be provided with one. I have read this Shipwrecked Seaman's Manual with a melancholy kind of interest,—for the sound of the surf, or, you might say, the moaning of the sea, is heard all through it, as if its author were the sole survivor of a shipwreck himself. Of this part of the coast he says:

"This highland approaches the ocean with steep and lofty banks, which it is extremely difficult to climb, especially in a storm. In violent tempests, during very high tides, the sea breaks against the foot of them, rendering it then unsafe to walk on the strand which lies between them and the ocean. Should the seaman succeed in his attempt to ascend them, he must forbear to penetrate into the country, as houses are generally so remote that they would escape his research during the night; he must pass on to the valleys by which the banks are intersected. These valleys, which the inhabitants call Hollows, run at right angles with the shore, and in the middle or lowest part of them a road leads from the dwelling-houses to the sea."

By the word *road* must not always be understood a visible cart-track. There were these two roads for us,—an upper and a lower one,—the bank and the beach; both stretching twenty-eight miles northwest, from Nauset Harbor to Race Point, without a single opening into the beach, and with hardly a serious interruption of the desert. If you were to ford the narrow and shallow inlet at Nauset Harbor, where there is not more than eight feet of water on the bar at full sea, you might walk ten or twelve miles farther, which would make a beach forty miles long,—and the bank and beach, on the east side of Nantucket, are but a continuation of these.

I was comparatively satisfied. There I had got the Cape under me, as much as if I were riding it bare-backed. It was not as on the map, or seen from the stage-coach; but there I found it all out of doors, huge and real, Cape Cod! as it cannot be represented on a map, color it as you will; the thing itself, than which there is nothing more like it, no truer picture or account; which you cannot go farther and see. I cannot remember what I thought before that it was. They commonly celebrate those beaches only which have a hotel on them, not those which have a humane house alone. But I wished to see that seashore where man's works are wrecks; to put up at the true Atlantic House, where the ocean is land-lord as well as sea-lord, and comes ashore without a wharf for the landing; where the crumbling land is the only invalid, or at best is but dry land, and that is all you can say of it.

☙ Salvage

Before the construction of the Cape Cod Canal made it unnecessary to sail around the length of the Cape, wrecking, as it was called, was an important part of the Cape's economy. The wreckers wandered up and down the beaches to see what they could salvage from the sea, picking up odd pieces of rope and lumber and occasionally more significant items. This was the business's most innocent form. In other instances, the wreckers would go to the scene of an actual shipwreck and, after some effort to save the crew, would divide the cargo among themselves. In order to bring it ashore they sometimes used poles; and the story is told in one town that the men agreed among themselves to limit the length of their poles to ten feet so that one would not have an advantage over another. The minister, however, as a perquisite of office, was permitted a twenty-foot pole.

The most serious type of wrecking, here as elsewhere along the coast, involved mounting false signals on the shore to lure vessels aground deliberately. On Cape Cod, those engaged in such work were called *mooncussers,* because they could not operate as effectively on moonlit nights as on nights that were completely dark. Some apologists for Cape Cod maintain that such purposeful wrecking never took place on the Cape, but the stories still persist.

✦ As we were walking close to the water's edge this morning, we turned round, by chance, and saw a large black object which the waves had just cast up on the beach behind us, yet too far off for us to distinguish what it was; and when we were about to return to it, two men came running from the bank, where no human beings had appeared before, as if they had come out of the sand, in order to save it before another wave took it. As we approached, it took successively the form of a huge fish, a drowned man, a sail or a net, and finally of a mass of tow-cloth, part of the cargo of the Franklin,[1] which the men loaded into a cart.

. . . . .

Objects on the beach, whether men or inanimate things, look not only exceedingly grotesque, but much larger and more wonderful than they actually are. Lately, when approaching the seashore several degrees south of this, I saw before me, seemingly half a mile distant, what appeared like bold and rugged cliffs on the beach, fifteen feet high, and whitened by the sun and waves; but after a few steps it proved to be low heaps of rags,—part of the cargo of a wrecked vessel,—scarcely more than a foot in height.

. . . . .

From time to time we saved a wreck ourselves, a box or barrel, and set it on its end, and appropriated it with crossed sticks; and it will lie there perhaps, respected by brother wreckers, until some more violent storm shall take it, really lost to man until wrecked again. We also saved, at the cost of wet feet only, a valuable cord and buoy, part of a seine, with

[1 A ship that had recently been wrecked off the Cape Cod coast.—A.B.A.]

which the sea was playing for it seemed ungracious to refuse the least gift which so great a personage offered you. We brought this home and still use it for a garden line.

I picked up a bottle half buried in the wet sand, covered with barnacles, but stoppled tight, and half full of red ale, which still smacked of juniper,—all that remained I fancied from the wreck of a rowdy world,—that great salt sea on the one hand, and this little sea of ale on the other, preserving their separate characters. What if it could tell us its adventures over countless ocean waves! Man would not be man through such ordeals as it had passed. But as I poured it slowly out on to the sand, it seemed to me that man himself was like a half-emptied bottle of pale ale, which Time had drunk so far, yet stoppled tight for a while, and drifting about in the ocean of circumstances, but destined erelong to mingle with the surrounding waves, or be spilled amid the sands of a distant shore.

⋐ Kelp

Kelps, which so fascinated Thoreau, are, of course, brown algae. Like most seaweeds, they are composed of three parts: a root that serves merely to keep the plant anchored and does not assist in its nourishment, a stem, and a leaf. In order to survive the tremendous forces of the ocean currents, kelp must anchor itself to a rock and not simply bury its roots in the sand, as a land plant would do. The brown color is caused by a pigment that covers up the green of the chlorophyll. Particularly after a heavy storm, many of these seaweeds are torn loose from the bottom and cast up on the shore. They can be found by searching the edge of the water and by rummaging through the tide wrack.

⋐ There was but little weed cast up here, and that kelp chiefly, there being scarcely a rock for rock-weed to adhere to. Who has not had a vision from some vessel's deck, when he had still his land legs on, of this great brown apron, drifting half upright, and quite submerged through the green water, clasping a stone or a deep-sea mussel in its unearthly fingers? I have seen it carrying a stone half as large as my head. We sometimes watched a mass of this cable-like weed, as it was tossed up on the crest of a breaker, waiting with interest to see it come in, as if there was some treasure buoyed up by it; but we were always surprised and disappointed at the insignificance of the mass which had attracted us. As we looked out over the water, the smallest objects floating on it appeared indefinitely large, we were so impressed by the vastness of the ocean, and each one bore so large a proportion to the whole ocean, which we saw. We were so often disappointed in the size of such things as came ashore, the ridiculous bits of wood or weed, with which the ocean labored, that we began to doubt whether the Atlantic itself would bear a still closer inspection, and would not turn out to be but a small pond, if it should come ashore to us.

This kelp, oar-weed, tangle, devil's apron, sole-leather, or ribbon-weed,—as various species are called,—appeared to us a singularly marine and fabulous product, a fit invention for Neptune to adorn his car with, or a freak of Proteus. All that is told of the sea has a fabulous sound to an inhabitant of the land, and all its products have a certain fabulous quality, as if they belonged to another planet, from seaweed to a sailor's yarn, or a fish story. In this element the animal and vegetable kingdoms meet and are strangely mingled. One species of kelp, according to Bory St. Vincent, has a stem fifteen hundred feet long, and hence is the longest vegetable known, and a brig's crew spent two days to no purpose collecting the trunks of another kind cast ashore on the Falkland Islands, mistaking it for drift-wood.

This species looked almost edible; at least, I thought that if I were starving, I would try it. One sailor told me that the cows ate it. It cut like cheese; for I took the earliest opportunity to sit down and deliberately whittle up a fathom or two of it, that I might become more intimately acquainted with it, see how it cut, and if it were hollow all the way through. The blade looked like a broad belt, whose edges had been quilled, or as if stretched by hammering, and it was also

28

twisted spirally. The extremity was generally worn and ragged from the lashing of the waves. A piece of the stem which I carried home shrunk to one quarter of its size a week afterward, and was completely covered with crystals of salt like frost. The reader will excuse my greenness,—though it is not sea-greenness, like his, perchance,—for I live by a river shore, where this weed does not wash up. When we consider in what meadows it grew, and how it was raked, and in what kind of hay weather got in or out, we may well be curious about it.

. . . . .

The beach was also strewn with beautiful sea-jellies, which the wreckers called sun-squall, one of the lowest forms of animal life, some white, some wine-colored, and a foot in diameter. I at first thought that they were a tender part of some marine monster, which the storm or some other foe had mangled. What right has the sea to bear in its bosom such tender things as sea-jellies and mosses, when it has such a boisterous shore, that the stoutest fabric are wrecked against it? Strange that it should undertake to dandle such delicate children in its arm. I did not at first recognize these for the same which I had formerly seen in myriads in Boston Harbor, rising, with a waving motion, to the surface, as if to meet the sun, and discoloring the waters far and wide, so that I seemed to be sailing through a mere sun-fish soup. They say that when you endeavor to take one up, it will spill out the other side of your hand like quicksilver.

Gulls and Other Birds

Blackbirds and crows were once so common on the Cape that Eastham set a quota for each male resident to kill annually. If a man failed to meet his quota, he was fined. Bachelors had a particularly difficult time of it, because they could not obtain permission to be married unless they had killed the proper number of birds. Such practices, of course, have long since stopped. The visitor today, if he has a special interest in birds, should visit the spit of land at the mouth of Nauset Harbor. While this spit can be conveniently observed by going to the settlement of Nauset Heights, the confirmed "birder" will want to get nearer. This can be done by going from Eastham to the Nauset Coast Guard Beach, leaving the car in the parking lot, and walking south. Shore birds tend to congregate in the flats and shallows that will appear to the right. Farther along on his trip the visitor may wish to stop at the Audubon Sanctuary in Wellfleet. Its entrance is marked by a sign, and it lies to the left on Route 6 going toward Provincetown. Also, while visiting the Highland Light in Truro, he should take time to observe the bank swallows, which still nest in holes in the bank as they did in Thoreau's day.

Before the land rose out of the ocean, and became *dry* land, chaos reigned; and between high and low water mark, where she is partially disrobed and rising, a sort of chaos reigns still, which only anomalous creatures can inhabit. Mackerel-gulls[1] were all the while flying over our heads and amid the breakers, sometimes two white ones pursuing a black one; quite at home in the storm, though they are as delicate organizations as sea-jellies and mosses; and we saw that they were adapted to their circumstances rather by their spirits than their bodies. Theirs must be an essentially wilder, that is less human, nature, than that of larks and robins. Their note was like the sound of some vibrating metal, and harmonized well with the scenery and the roar of the surf, as if one had rudely touched the strings of the lyre, which ever lies on the shore; a ragged shred of ocean music tossed aloft on the spray.

But if I were required to name a sound, the remembrance of which most perfectly revives the impression which the beach has made, it would be the dreary peep of the piping plover (*Charadrius melodus*) which haunts there. Their voices, too, are heard as a fugacious part in the dirge which is ever played along the shore for those mariners who have been lost in the deep since first it was created. But through all this dreariness we seemed to have a pure and unqualified strain of eternal melody, for always the same strain which is a dirge to one household is a morning song of rejoicing to another.

A remarkable method of catching gulls, derived from the Indians, was practiced in Wellfleet in 1794. "The Gull House," it is said, "is built with crotchets, fixed in the ground on the beach," poles being stretched across for the top, and the sides made close with stakes and seaweed. "The poles on the top are covered with lean whale. The man, being placed within, is not discovered by the fowls, and, while they are contending for and eating the flesh, he draws them in, one by one, be-

[1 Mackerel gulls are terns and most generally the common tern.—A.B.A.]

tween the poles, until he has collected forty or fifty." Hence, perchance, a man is said to be *gulled*, when he is *taken in.*

We read that one "sort of gulls is called by the Dutch *malle-mucke, i.e.*, the foolish fly, because they fall upon a whale as eagerly as a fly, and, indeed, all gulls are foolishly bold and easy to be shot. The Norwegians call this bird *havhest*, sea-horse (and the English translator says, it is probably what we call boobies). If they have eaten too much, they throw it up, and eat it again till they are tired. It is this habit in the gulls of parting with their property [disgorging the contents of their stomachs to the skuas], which has given rise to the terms gull, guller, and gulling, among men."

We also read that they used to kill small birds which roosted on the beach at night, by making a fire with hog's lard in a frying-pan. The Indians probably used pine torches; the birds flocked to the light, and were knocked down with a stick. We noticed holes dug near the edge of the bank, where gunners conceal themselves to shoot the large gulls which coast up and down a-fishing, for these are considered good to eat.

. . . . .

Some times we sat on the wet beach and watched the beach birds, sand-pipers, and others, trotting along close to each wave, and waiting for the sea to cast up their breakfast. The former (*Charadrius melodus*) ran with great rapidity, and then stood stock still, remarkably erect, and hardly to be distinguished from the beach. The wet sand was covered with small skipping Sea Fleas, which apparently made a part of their food. These last are the little scavengers of the beach, and are so numerous that they will devour large fishes, which have been cast up, in a very short time. One little bird not larger than a sparrow—it may have been a Phalarope—would alight on the turbulent surface where the breakers were five or six feet high, and float buoyantly there like a duck, cunningly taking to its wings and lifting itself a few feet through the air over the foaming crest of each breaker, but sometimes outriding safely a considerable billow which hid it some seconds, when its instinct told it that it would not break. It was a little creature thus to sport with the ocean, but it was as perfect a success in its way as the breakers in theirs. There was also an almost uninterrupted line of coots rising and falling with the waves, a few rods from the shore, the whole length of the Cape. They made as constant a part of the ocean's border as the pads or pickerel-weed do of that of a pond.

The Woods of Eastham

It is almost impossible to give formal directions for exploring this part of the Cape and some of the other general areas that Thoreau describes. The visitor should remember that Route 6 continues down the center of the Cape until Provincetown. Regardless of how the Cape bends around on itself—it forms almost a complete circle—Cape Cod Bay will lie on his left and the Back-side—the open Atlantic—will lie on his right. Generally speaking, the Back-side will be wilder and more desolate, because the early colonists tended to found their towns on the Bay side, that is, the side on Cape Cod Bay. It was the Back-side, however, which most appealed to Thoreau. Continuing up Route 6, the visitor can take side excursions down the numerous roads that open from Route 6, depending on the amount of time at his disposal. He should, however, beware of unpaved roads and the shoulders of those that are paved; many of them are so sandy that if he gets onto one he will need to call a tow truck to free his car. This becomes more of a hazard the nearer he comes to Provincetown.

When we have returned from the seaside, we sometimes ask ourselves why we did not spend more time in gazing at the sea; but very soon the traveler does not look at the sea more than at the heavens. As for the interior, if the elevated sand-bar in the midst of the ocean can be said to have any interior, it was an exceedingly desolate landscape, with rarely a cultivated or cultivable field in sight. We saw no villages, and seldom a house, for these are generally on the Bay side. It was a succession of shrubby hills and valleys, now wearing an autumnal tint. You would frequently think, from the character of the surface, the dwarfish trees, and the bearberries around, that you were on the top of a mountain.

The only wood in Eastham was on the edge of Wellfleet. The pitch-pines were not commonly more than fifteen or eighteen feet high. The larger ones were covered with lichens, —often hung with the long gray *Usnea*. There is scarcely a white-pine on the forearm of the Cape. Yet in the northwest part of Eastham, near the Camp Ground,[1] we saw, the next summer, some quite rural, and even sylvan retreats, for the Cape, where small rustling groves of oaks and locusts and whispering pines, on perfectly level ground, made a little paradise. The locusts, both transplanted and growing naturally about the houses there, appeared to flourish better than any other tree. There were thin belts of wood in Wellfleet and Truro, a mile or more from the Atlantic, but, for the most part, we could see the horizon through them, or if extensive, the trees were not large. Both oaks and pines had often the same flat look with the apple-trees. Commonly, the oak woods twenty-five years old were a mere scraggy shrubbery nine or ten feet high, and we could frequently reach to their topmost leaf. Much that is called "woods" was about half as high as this,—only patches of shrub-oak, bayberry, beach-plum, and wild roses, overrun with woodbine.

[1 So named because prayer meetings were once held there.—A.B.A.]

When the roses were in bloom, these patches in the midst of the sand displayed such a profusion of blossoms, mingled with the aroma of the bayberry, that no Italian or other artificial rose-garden could equal them. They were perfectly Elysian, and realized my idea of an oasis in the desert. Huckleberry bushes were very abundant, and the next summer they bore a remarkable quantity of that kind of gall called Huckleberry-apple, forming quite handsome though monstrous blossoms.

. . . . .

Every landscape which is dreary enough has a certain beauty to my eyes, and in this instance its permanent qualities were enhanced by the weather. Everything told of the sea, even when we did not see its waste or hear its roar. For birds there were gulls, and for carts in the fields, boats turned bottom upward against the houses, and sometimes the rib of a whale was woven into the fence by the roadside.[2] The trees were, if possible, rarer than the houses, excepting apple-trees, of which there were a few small orchards in the hollows. These were either narrow and high, with flat tops, having lost their side branches, like huge plum-bushes growing in exposed situations, or else dwarfed and branching immediately at the ground, like quince-bushes. They suggested that, under like circumstances, all trees would at last acquire like habits of growth. I afterward saw on the Cape many full-grown apple-trees not higher than a man's head; one whole orchard, indeed, where all the fruit could have been gathered by a man standing on the ground; but you could hardly creep beneath the trees.

Some, which the owners told me were twenty years old, were only three and a half feet high, spreading at six inches from the ground five feet each way, and being withal surrounded with boxes of tar to catch the canker-worms, they looked like plants in flower-pots, and as if they might be taken into the house in the winter. In another place, I saw some not

[2 The jawbones of a whale still form a gateway to the Penniman house in Eastham.—A.B.A.]

much larger than currant-bushes; yet the owner told me that they had borne a barrel and a half of apples that fall. If they had been placed close together, I could have cleared them all at a jump. I measured some near the Highland Light in Truro, which had been taken from the shrubby woods thereabouts when young, and grafted. One, which had been set ten years, was on an average eighteen inches high, and spread nine feet, with a flat top. It had borne one bushel of apples two years before. Another, probably twenty years old from the seed, was five feet high, and spread eighteen feet, branching, as usual, at the ground, so that you could not creep under it. This bore a barrel of apples two years before.

The owner of these trees invariably used the personal pronoun in speaking of them; as, "I got *him* out of the woods, but *he* doesn't bear." The largest that I saw in that neighborhood was nine feet high to the topmost leaf, and spread thirty-three feet, branching at the ground five ways. In one yard I observed a single, very healthy-looking tree, while all the rest were dead or dying. The occupant said that his father had manured all but that one with blackfish.

. . . . .

The inhabitants of these towns have a great regard for a tree, though their standard for one is necessarily neither large nor high; and when they tell you of the large trees that once grew here, you must think of them, not as absolutely large, but large compared with the present generation. Their "brave old oaks," of which they speak with so much respect, and which they will point out to you as relics of the primitive forest, one hundred or one hundred and fifty, ay, for aught they know, two hundred years old, have a ridiculously dwarfish appearance, which excites a smile in the beholder. The largest and most venerable which they will show you in such a case are, perhaps, not more than twenty or twenty-five feet high. I was especially amused by the Lilliputian old oaks in the south part of Truro. To the inexperienced eye, which appreciated their proportions only, they might appear vast as the tree which saved his royal majesty, but measured they were dwarfed at once almost into lichens which a deer might eat up in a morning.

Yet they will tell you that large schooners were once built of timber which grew in Wellfleet. The old houses also are built of the timber of the Cape; but instead of the forests in the midst of which they originally stood, barren heaths, with poverty-grass for heather, now stretch away on every side. The modern houses are built of what is called "dimension timber," imported from Maine, all ready to be set up, so that commonly they do not touch it again with an axe. Almost all the wood used for fuel is *imported* by vessels or currents, and of course all the coal. I was told that probably a quarter of the fuel and a considerable part of the lumber used in North Truro was drift-wood. Many get *all* their fuel from the beach.

The Table Lands of Eastham

Although called the Table Lands of Eastham, this section, as Thoreau points out, is part of Wellfleet. The visitor will undoubtedly be frustrated by the fact that as he enters Wellfleet he cannot turn right off Route 6 because the area is occupied by a military reservation; the first turn he can take will be somewhat farther down the road and will bring him to Wellfleet by the Sea, a modern summer community which is worth visiting because of the view it gives of the ocean. In fact, a road called Ocean View Drive runs along the shore at this point. By following it for some distance and then turning left on Long Pond Road, the visitor will have a good sight of the ocean and eventually find himself back on Route 6. A short distance farther on he can again turn to the right, on Gross Hill Road. This will lead past Gull Pond, which will be on the left. Thoreau is said to have once spent the night just north of here, on a knoll overlooking Williams Pond.

The wrecker directed us to a slight depression, called Snow's Hollow, by which we ascended the bank,—for elsewhere, if not difficult, it was inconvenient to climb it on ac-

41

count of the sliding sand which filled our shoes. This sand-bank—the backbone of the Cape—rose directly from the beach to the height of a hundred feet or more above the ocean. It was with singular emotions that we first stood upon it and discovered what a place we had chosen to walk on. On our right, beneath us, was the beach of smooth and gently-sloping sand, a dozen rods in width; next, the endless series of white breakers; further still, the light green water over the bar, which runs the whole length of the fore-arm of the Cape, and beyond this stretched the unwearied and illimitable ocean. On our left, extending back from the very edge of the bank, was a perfect desert of shining sand, from thirty to eighty rods in width, skirted in the distance by small sand-hills fifteen or twenty feet high; between which, however, in some places, the sand penetrated as much farther.

Next commenced the region of vegetation,—a succession of small hills and valleys covered with shrubbery, now glowing with the brightest imaginable autumnal tints; and beyond this were seen, here and there, the waters of the bay. Here, in Wellfleet, this pure sand plateau, known to sailors as the Table Lands of Eastham, on account of its appearance, as seen from the ocean, and because it once made a part of that town, —full fifty rods in width, and in many places much more, and sometimes full one hundred and fifty feet above the ocean, —stretched away northward from the southern boundary of the town, without a particle of vegetation,—as level almost as a table,—for two and a half or three miles, or as far as the eye could reach; slightly rising towards the ocean, then stooping to the beach, by as steep a slope as sand could lie on, and as regular as a military engineer could desire. It was like the escarped rampart of a stupendous fortress, whose glacis was the beach, and whose champaign the ocean.

From its surface we overlooked the greater part of the Cape. In short, we were traversing a desert, with the view of an autumnal landscape of extraordinary brilliancy, a sort of Promised Land, on the one hand, and the ocean on the other. Yet,

42

though the prospect was so extensive, and the country for the most part destitute of trees, a house was rarely visible,—we never saw one from the beach,—and the solitude was that of the ocean and the desert combined. A thousand men could not have seriously interrupted it, but would have been lost in the vastness of the scenery as their footsteps in the sand.

The Sound of the Ocean

By this time, if the sea is at all rough, the visitor will be as conscious as Thoreau was of its constant roar and will enjoy Thoreau's description. Then, as a contrast, he will want to visit the town of Wellfleet, which lies on the other side of Route 6. There are plentiful road signs, and consequently it is easy to reach. Its quiet, well-protected harbor is directly the opposite of what the visitor has seen on the Back-side. Here the fishing boats come in each evening to take shelter, winding down the narrow channel between the flats, which are completely exposed at low tide. Wellfleet's principal industry for many years was oysters, and the town also played an important role in starting another important American business: Captain Lorenzo Dow Baker, a Wellfleet resident, brought the first commercial cargo of bananas from South America to Boston in 1871. He later formed the L. D. Baker Company, which eventually became the United Fruit Company.

The sounds which the ocean makes must be very significant and interesting to those who live near it. When I was leaving the shore at this place the next summer, and had got a quarter of a mile distant, ascending a hill, I was startled by a sudden,

45

loud sound from the sea, as if a large steamer were letting off steam by the shore, so that I caught my breath and felt my blood run cold for an instant, and I turned about, expecting to see one of the Atlantic steamers thus far out of her course, but there was nothing unusual to be seen.

There was a low bank at the entrance of the Hollow, between me and the ocean, and suspecting that I might have risen into another stratum of air in ascending the hill,—which had wafted to me only the ordinary roar of the sea,—I immediately descended again, to see if I lost hearing of it; but without regard to my ascending or descending, it died away in a minute or two, and yet there was scarcely any wind all the while. The old man said that this was what they called the "rut," a peculiar roar of the sea before the wind changes, which, however, he could not account for. He thought that he could tell all about the weather from the sounds which the sea made.

Old Josselyn, who came to New England in 1638, has it among his weather-signs, that "the resounding of the sea from the shore, and murmuring of the winds in the woods, without apparent wind, sheweth wind to follow."

Being on another part of the coast one night since this, I heard the roar of the surf a mile distant, and the inhabitants said it was a sign that the wind would work round east, and we should have rainy weather. The ocean was heaped up somewhere at the eastward, and this roar was occasioned by its effort to preserve its equilibrium, the wave reaching the shore before the wind. Also the captain of a packet between this country and England told me that he sometimes met with a wave on the Atlantic coming against the wind, perhaps in a calm sea, which indicated that at a distance the wind was blowing from an opposite quarter, but the undulation had traveled faster than it. Sailors tell of "tide-rips" and "ground-swells," which they suppose to have been occasioned by hurricanes and earthquakes, and to have traveled many hundred, and sometimes even two or three thousand miles.

⋘ Bayberries

Bayberries are still common on the Cape, as they are through much of New England. The pewter molds in which bayberry candles were made can still be unearthed from time to time in antique shops, though they are becoming scarcer by the year. The candles themselves are still made and offered for sale at many of the roadside stands along Route 6. They are fairly expensive as candles go, but they give off a slight odor of bayberries as they burn and are a link between today and the past.

⋘ Our way to the high sand-bank, which I have described as extending all along the coast, led, as usual, through patches of bayberry bushes, which straggled into the sand. This, next to the shrub-oak, was perhaps the most common shrub thereabouts. I was much attracted by its odoriferous leaves and small gray berries which are clustered about the short twigs, just below the last year's growth. I know of but two bushes in Concord, and they, being staminate plants, do not bear fruit. The berries gave it a venerable appearance, and they smelled quite spicy, like small confectionery. Robert Beverley, in his "History of Virginia," published in 1705, states that:

"At the mouth of their rivers, and all along upon the sea and bay, and near many of their creeks and swamps, grows the myrtle, bearing a berry, of which they make a hard, brittle wax, of a curious green color, which by refining becomes almost transparent. Of this they make candles, which are never greasy to the touch nor melt with lying in the hottest weather; neither does the snuff of these ever offend the smell, like that of a tallow candle; but, instead of being disagreeable, if an accident puts a candle out, it yields a pleasant fragrancy to all that are in the room; insomuch that nice people often put them out on purpose to have the incense of the expiring snuff. The melting of these berries is said to have been first found out by a surgeon in New England, who performed wonderful things with a salve made of them."

From the abundance of berries still hanging on the bushes, we judged that the inhabitants did not generally collect them for tallow, though we had seen a piece in the house we had just left. I have since made some tallow myself. Holding a basket beneath the bare twigs in April, I rubbed them together between my hands and thus gathered about a quart in twenty minutes, to which were added enough to make three pints, and I might have gathered them much faster with a suitable rake and a large shallow basket. They have little prominences like those of an orange all creased in tallow, which also fills the interstices down to the stone. The oily part rose to the top, making it look like a savory black broth, which smelled much like balm or other herb tea. You let it cool, then skim off the tallow from the surface, melt this again and strain it. I got about a quarter of a pound weight from my three pints, and more yet remained within the berries. A small portion cooled in the form of small flattish hemispheres, like crystallizations, the size of a kernel of corn—nuggets I called them as I picked them out from amid the berries. Loudon says, that "cultivated trees are said to yield more wax than those that are found wild." If you get any pitch on your hands in the pine-woods you have only to rub some of these berries between your hands to start it off.

⤟ Truro

Truro was one of the areas on the Lower Cape that was explored by the Pilgrims before they settled at Plymouth. Here at Corn Hill, which lies on Cape Cod Bay just north of the town, the Pilgrims discovered hillocks of freshly heaped sand, and when they dug into them, they found a supply of corn that the Indians had cached. The Pilgrims took this corn with them and later used it as seed, and it played an important role in preventing the Plymouth Colony from starving. In 1700 a group of settlers moved to Truro from Eastham, and it was incorporated as a town in 1709. At one time it was an important fishing center with sixty-three fishing boats going out from its harbor. It also had an extensive ship-building business and salt works.

⤟ To-day we were walking through Truro, a town of about eighteen hundred inhabitants. We had already come to Pamet River, which empties into the Bay. This was the limit of the Pilgrims' journey up the Cape from Provincetown, when seeking a place for settlement. It rises in a hollow within a few rods of the Atlantic, and one who lives near its source told us that in high tides the sea leaked through, yet the wind and waves preserve intact the barrier between them, and thus the whole river is steadily driven westward butt-end foremost,—fountain-head, channel, and light-house, at the mouth, all together.

. . . . .

After arranging to lodge at the light-house, we rambled across the Cape to the Bay, over a singularly bleak and barren-looking country, consisting of rounded hills and hollows, called by geologists diluvial elevations and depressions,—a kind of scenery which has been compared to a chopped sea, though this suggests too sudden a transition. There is a delineation of this very landscape in Hitchcock's Report on the Geology of Massachusetts, a work which, by it size at least, reminds one of a diluvial elevation itself. Looking southward from the light-house, the Cape appeared like an elevated plateau, sloping very regularly, though slightly, downward from the edge of the bank on the Atlantic side, about one hundred and fifty feet above the ocean, to that on the Bay side. On traversing this we found it to be interrupted by broad valleys or gullies, which become the hollows in the bank when the sea has worn up to them. They are commonly at right angles with the shore, and often extend quite across the Cape.

. . . . .

Some of the valleys, however, are circular, a hundred feet deep, without any outlet, as if the Cape had sunk in those places, or its sands had run out. The few scattered houses which we passed, being placed at the bottom of the hollows, for shelter and fertility, were, for the most part, concealed entirely, as much as if they had been swallowed up in the earth. Even a village with its meeting-house, which we had left little more than a stone's throw behind, had sunk into the earth, spire and all, and we saw only the surface of the upland and the sea on either hand. When approaching it, we had mistaken the belfry for a summer-house on the plain. We began to think that we might tumble into a village before we were aware of it, as into an ant-lion's hole, and be drawn into the sand irrecoverably. The most conspicuous objects on the land were a distant windmill, or a meeting-house standing alone, for only they could afford to occupy an exposed place. A great part of the township, however, is a barren, heath-like plain, and perhaps one third of it lies in common, though the property of individuals.

The author of the old "Description of Truro," speaking of the soil, says, "The snow, which would be of essential service to it provided it lay level and covered the ground, is blown into drifts and into the sea."

This peculiar open country, with here and there a patch of shrubbery, extends as much as seven miles, or from Pamet River on the south to High Head on the north, and from Ocean to Bay. To walk over it makes on a stranger such an impression as being at sea, and he finds it impossible to estimate distances in any weather. A windmill or a herd of cows may seem to be far away in the horizon, yet, after going a few rods, he will be close upon them. He is also deluded by other kinds of mirage. When, in the summer, I saw a family a-blueberrying a mile off, walking about amid the dwarfish bushes which did not come up higher than their ankles, they seemed to me to be a race of giants, twenty feet high at least.

The Highland Light

In 1794, the Reverend Levi Whitman of Wellfleet suggested the construction of a lighthouse at this point. The offshore shoals make the waters here dangerous, and the height of the bank provides good visibility. It can be imagined, however, that not all Cape Codders were enthusiastic about the project, for it would interfere with their usual business of salvaging shipwrecks. In 1797 the government purchased ten acres and constructed the original lighthouse, which was the one that Thoreau saw. Because this light is the first to be seen by ships coming to Boston from Europe, it has always been important to navigators. It was rebuilt in 1857. One mile to the northeast are the Peaked Hill Bars, where many ships have been wrecked. One of these was the British man-of-war *Somerset*, which is mentioned in Longfellow's "Paul Revere's Ride." Four hundred and eighty members of her crew were captured by triumphant Cape Codders and marched to Boston. The fact that for two years the ship had been stationed off the Cape Cod coast and had harassed the inhabitants only added to the pleasure of their revenge. Standing near the lighthouse today and looking over the Highlands Golf Course, the visitor can see the

55

North Truro Air Force Station. About half a mile away in
the same direction is a curious structure that looks like an
English castle. It actually is part of the old Fitchburg
Railroad Station that was erected in Boston in 1847. When
the station was torn down in 1927, a Boston attorney
brought this tower to Truro.

◄▓◄ This light-house, known to mariners as the Cape Cod or
Highland Light, is one of our "primary sea-coast lights," and
is usually the first seen by those approaching the entrance of
Massachusetts Bay from Europe. It is forty-three miles from
Cape Ann Light, and forty-one from Boston Light. It stands
about twenty rods from the edge of the bank, which is here
formed of clay. I borrowed the plane and square, level and
dividers, of a carpenter who was shingling a barn near by,
and, using one of those shingles made of a mast, contrived a
rude sort of quadrant, with pins for sights and pivots, and got
the angle of elevation of the Bank opposite the light-house,
and with a couple of codlines the length of its slope, and so
measured its height on the shingle.

It rises one hundred and ten feet above its immediate base,
or about one hundred and twenty-three feet above mean low
water. Graham, who has carefully surveyed the extremity of
the Cape, makes it one hundred and thirty feet. The mixed
sand and clay lay at an angle of forty degrees with the horizon,
where I measured it, but the clay is generally much steeper.
No cow nor hen ever gets down it. Half a mile farther south the
bank is fifteen or twenty-five feet higher, and that appeared
to be the highest land in North Truro. Even this vast clay
bank is fast wearing away. Small streams of water trickling
down it at intervals of two or three rods, have left the inter-
mediate clay in the form of steep Gothic roofs fifty feet high
or more, the ridges as sharp and rugged-looking as rocks; and
in one place the bank is curiously eaten out in the form of a
large semi-circular crater.

56

According to the light-house keeper, the Cape is wasting here on both sides, though most on the eastern. In some places it has lost many rods within the last year, and, erelong, the light-house must be moved. We calculated, *from his data,* how soon the Cape would be quite worn away at this point, "for," said he, "I can remember sixty years back." We were even more surprised at this last announcement—that is, at the slow waste of life and energy in our informant, for we had taken him to be not more than forty—than at the rapid wasting of the Cape, and we thought that he stood a fair chance to outlive the former.

Between this October and June of the next year, I found that the bank had lost about forty feet in one place, opposite the light-house, and it was cracked more than forty feet farther from the edge at the last date, the shore being strewn with the recent rubbish. But I judged that generally it was not wearing away here at the rate of more than six feet annually. Any conclusions drawn from the observations of a few years, or one generation only, are likely to prove false, and the Cape may balk expectation by its durability. In some places even a wrecker's foot-path down the bank lasts several years. One old inhabitant told us that when the light-house was built, in 1798, it was calculated that it would stand forty-five years, allowing the bank to waste one length of fence each year, "but," said he, "there it is" (or rather another near the same site, about twenty rods from the edge of the bank).

· · · · ·

In this bank, above the clay, I counted in the summer, two hundred holes of the Bank Swallow within a space six rods long, and there were at least one thousand old birds within three times that distance, twittering over the surf. I had never associated them in my thoughts with the beach before. One little boy who had been a-birds'-nesting had got eighty swallows' eggs for his share! Tell it not to the Humane Society!

There were many young birds on the clay beneath, which had tumbled out and died. Also there were many Crow-blackbirds[1] hopping about in the dry fields, and the Upland Plover were breeding close by the light-house. The keeper had once cut off one's wing while mowing, as she sat on her eggs there. This is also a favorite resort for gunners in the fall to shoot the Golden Plover.

As around the shores of a pond are seen devil's-needles, butterflies, etc., so here, to my surprise, I saw at the same season great devil's-needles of a size proportionably larger, or nearly as big as my finger, incessantly coasting up and down the edge of the bank, and butterflies also were hovering over it, and I never saw so many dorr-bugs and beetles of various kinds as strewed the beach. They had apparently flown over the bank in the night, and could not get up again, and some had perhaps fallen into the sea and were washed ashore. They may have been in part attracted by the light-house lamps.

[1 A common name at that time for purple grackles.—A.B.A.]

ⵌ The Wind

In this section, Thoreau speaks of the sea playing with the land as a cat plays with a mouse. Anyone who has lived on the Cape for any length of time learns to recognize the way the sea has shaped and reshaped the entire coastline of the Cape. The casual visitor may have more difficulty, but if he goes swimming in the surf, he can feel the sand moving under his feet and through the water near him. He will begin to realize that the Cape is almost like a live thing, twisting and moving under the pressures of winds and waves.

ⵌ Over this bare Highland the wind has full sweep. Even in July it blows the wings over the heads of the young turkeys, which do not know enough to head against it; and in gales the doors and windows are blown in, and you must hold on to the light-house to prevent being blown into the Atlantic. They who merely keep out on the beach in a storm in the winter are sometimes rewarded by the Humane Society. If you would feel the full force of a tempest, take up your residence on the top of Mount Washington, or at the Highland Light, in Truro.

. . . . .

The light-house keeper said that when the wind blowed strong on to the shore, the waves ate fast into the bank, but when it blowed off they took no sand away; for in the former case the wind heaped up the surface of the water next to the beach, and to preserve its equilibrium a strong undertow immediately set back again into the sea which carried with it the sand and whatever else was in the way, and left the beach hard to walk on; but in the latter case the undertow set on, and carried the sand with it, so that it was particularly difficult for shipwrecked men to get to land when the wind blowed on to the shore, but easier when it blowed off. This undertow, meeting the next surface wave on the bar which itself has made, forms part of the dam over which the latter breaks, as over an upright wall.

The sea thus plays with the land holding a sand-bar in its mouth awhile before it swallows it, as a cat plays with a mouse; but the fatal gripe is sure to come at last. The sea sends its rapacious east wind to rob the land, but before the former has got far with its prey, the land sends its honest west wind to recover some of its own. But, according to Lieutenant Davis, the forms, extent, and distribution of sand-bars and banks are principally determined, not by winds and waves, but by tides.

Our host said that you would be surprised if you were on the beach when the wind blew a hurricane directly on to it, to see that none of the drift-wood came ashore, but all was carried directly northward and parallel with the shore as fast as a man can walk, by the inshore current, which sets strongly in that direction at flood tide. The strongest swimmers also are carried along with it, and never gain an inch toward the beach. Even a large rock has been moved half a mile northward along the beach. He assured us that the sea was never still on the back side of the Cape, but ran commonly as high as your head, so that a great part of the time you could not launch a boat there, and even in the calmest weather the waves run six or eight feet up the beach, though then you could get off on a plank.

The Clay Pounds

Another interesting description of the Clay Pounds, the geologic structure on which the Highland Light is built, is given by Edward Kendall in his *Travels through the Northern Parts of the United States,* published in 1809. He described it as "a remarkable vein of blue clay, or marl, not more than two hundred yards broad, where it terminates abruptly on the beach, and growing narrower as it recedes inland, where, at the distance of half a mile, it contracts itself to a point; on each side all the country is sand. This vein of clay or marl was long regarded as the proper place for a light-house on the coast; and its solidity, not less than the high level of its surface, recommend it for this purpose: it is not, however, without a serious inconvenience. The impenetrable nature of the soil occasions the vapours that strike against it to remain on its surface."

The Clay Pounds are a more fertile tract than usual. We saw some fine patches of roots and corn here. As generally on the Cape, the plants had little stalk or leaf, but ran remarkably to seed. The corn was hardly more than half as high as in the interior, yet the ears were large and full, and one farmer told us that he could raise forty bushels on an acre without manure, and sixty with it. The heads of the rye also were remarkably large. The Shadbush (*Amelanchier*), Beach Plums, and Blueberries (*Vaccinium Pennsylvanicum*), like the apple-trees and oaks, were very dwarfish, spreading over the sand, but at the same time very fruitful. The blueberry was but an inch or two high, and its fruit often rested on the ground, so that you did not suspect the presence of the bushes, even on those bare hills, until you were treading on them.

I thought that this fertility must be owing mainly to the abundance of moisture in the atmosphere, for I observed that what little grass there was was remarkably laden with dew in the morning, and in summer dense imprisoning fogs frequently last till midday, turning one's beard into a wet napkin about his throat, and the oldest inhabitant may lose his way within a stone's throw of his house or be obliged to follow the beach for a guide. The brick house attached to the light-house was exceedingly damp at that season, and writing-paper lost all its stiffness in it. It was impossible to dry your towel after bathing, or to press flowers without their mildewing. The air was so moist that we rarely wished to drink, though we could at all times taste the salt on our lips. Salt was rarely used at table, and our host told us that his cattle invariably refused it when it was offered them, they got so much with their grass and at every breath, but he said that a sick horse or one just from the country would sometimes take a hearty draught of salt water, and seemed to like it and be the better for it.

It was surprising to see how much water was contained in the terminal bud of the seaside golden-rod, standing in the sand early in July, and also how turnips, beets, carrots, etc., flourished even in pure sand. A man traveling by the shore near there not long before us noticed something green growing in the pure sand of the beach, just at high-water mark, and on approaching found it to be a bed of beets flourishing vigorously, probably from seed washed out of the Franklin. Also beets and turnips came up in the seaweed used for manure in many parts of the Cape. This suggests how various plants may have been dispersed over the world to distant islands and continents.

Looking from the Beach

As Thoreau points out, the visitor looking seaward from this part of the Cape is gazing directly at Spain; between him and Europe there is no other land. In the creation of waves, one important factor is the "fetch," or the distance that the wave can be driven by the wind without hitting an obstacle. From the beach, the fetch is a long one, if the wind happens to be blowing onshore. As the waves pass out of the storm area, they begin to slow down and become a swell. These move across the ocean until they reach the shoals of Cape Cod, which slow them even more. As the waves behind overtake them, their height increases and they come tumbling down upon the beach. The visitor watching the waves can make an educated guess as to whether they were formed by a nearby storm or one far out at sea. If they are sharply shaped before reaching the beach, they are probably newly created; if, on the other hand, they are smooth and rounded until they pile up on the shoals, they have probably resulted from a storm hundreds of miles away.

Again we took to the beach for another day . . . walking along the shore of the resounding sea, determined to get it into us. We wished to associate with the Ocean until it lost the pond-like look which it wears to a countryman. We still thought that we could see the other side. Its surface was still more sparkling than the day before, and we beheld "the countless smilings of the ocean waves;" though some of them were pretty broad grins, for still the wind blew and the billows broke in foam along the beach. The nearest beach to us on the other side, whither we looked, due east, was on the coast of Galicia, in Spain, whose capital is Santiago, though by old poets' reckoning it should have been Atlantis or the Hesperides; but heaven is found to be farther west now. At first we were abreast of that part of Portugal *entre Douro e Mino,* and then Galicia and the port of Pontevedra opened to us as we walked along; but we did not enter, the breakers ran so high. The bold headland of Cape Finisterre, a little north of east, jutted toward us next, with its vain brag, for we flung back,—"Here is Cape Cod,—Cape Land's-Beginning." A little indentation toward the north,—for the land loomed to our imaginations by a common mirage,—we knew was the Bay of Biscay, and we sang:—

> "There we lay, till next day,
> In the Bay of Biscay O!"

A little south of east was Palos, where Columbus weighed anchor, and farther yet the pillars which Hercules set up; concerning which when we inquired at the top of our voices what was written on them,—for we had the morning sun in our faces, and could not see distinctly,—the inhabitants shouted *Ne plus ultra* (no more beyond), but the wind bore to us the truth only, *plus ultra* (more beyond), and over the Bay westward was echoed *ultra* (beyond). We spoke to them through the surf about the Far West, the true Hesperia, . . . [the] end of the day, the This Side Sundown, where the sun was extinguished in the *Pacific,* and we advised them to pull up stakes and plant those pillars of theirs on the shore of California, whither all our folks were gone,—the only *ne* plus ultra now. Whereat they looked crestfallen on their cliffs, for we had taken the wind out of all their sails. We could not perceive that any of their leavings washed up here, though we picked up a child's toy, a small dismantled boat, which may have been lost at Pontevedra.

~ The Ocean Again

As the visitor continues on his way toward Provincetown, he will find several side roads again opening onto Route 6 from the right. Several of these will lead into an area that was turned into a state park and therefore has few houses. Here, by following the signs that lead from Route 6, the visitor can find the spring where the Pilgrims were reputed to have drunk their first fresh water in the New World. It is marked by a monument and lies just at the edge of some salt meadows. A Boston doctor located it in 1920 after a considerable amount of research.

~ Still held on without a break the inland barrens and shrubbery, the desert and the high sand-bank with its even slope, the broad white beach, the breakers, the green water on the bar, and the Atlantic Ocean; and we traversed with delight new reaches of the shore; we took another lesson in sea-horses' manes and sea-cows' tails, in sea-jellies and sea-clams, with our new-gained experience. The sea ran hardly less than the day before. It seemed with every wave to be subsiding, because such was our expectation, and yet when hours had elapsed we could see no difference. But there it was, balancing itself, the restless ocean by our side, lurching in its gait. Each wave left the sand all braided or woven, as it were with a coarse woof and warp, and a distinct raised edge to its rapid work. We made no haste, since we wished to see the ocean at our leisure, and indeed that soft sand was no place in which to be in a hurry, for one mile there was as good as two elsewhere. Besides, we were obliged frequently to empty our shoes of the sand which one took in in climbing or descending the bank.

. . . . .

Though there were numerous vessels at this great distance in the horizon on every side, yet the vast spaces between them, like the spaces between the stars,—far as they were distant from us, so were they from one another—nay, some were twice as far from each other as from us,—impressed us with a sense of the immensity of the ocean, the "unfruitful ocean," as it has been called, and we could see what proportion man and his works bear to the globe. As we looked off, and saw the water growing darker and darker and deeper and deeper the farther we looked, till it was awful to consider, and it appeared to have no relation to the friendly land, either as shore or bottom—of what use is a bottom if it is out of sight, if it is two or three miles from the surface, and you are to be drowned so long before you get to it, though it were made of the same stuff with your native soil?— over that ocean where, as the Veda[1] says, "there is nothing to give support, nothing to rest upon, nothing to cling to," I felt that I was a land animal. The man in a balloon even may commonly alight on the earth in a few moments, but the sailor's only hope is that he may reach the distant shore. I could then appreciate the heroism of the old navigator, Sir Humphrey Gilbert, of whom it is related, that being overtaken by a storm when on his return from America, in the year 1583, far northeastward from where we were, sitting abaft with a book in his hand, just before he was swallowed up in the deep, he cried out to his comrades

[1 A sacred book of the Hindus.—A.B.A.]

72

in the Hind, as they came within hearing, "We are as near to Heaven by sea as by land." I saw that it would not be easy to realize.

. . . . .

. . . None of the elements were resting. On the beach there is a ceaseless activity, always something going on, in storm and in calm, winter and summer, night and day. Even the sedentary man here enjoys a breadth of view which is almost equivalent to motion. In clear weather the laziest may look across the Bay as far as Plymouth at a glance, or over the Atlantic as far as human vision reaches, merely raising his eyelids; or if he is too lazy to look after all, he can hardly help *hearing* the ceaseless dash and roar of the breakers. The restless ocean may at any moment cast up a whale or a wrecked vessel at your feet. All the reporters in the world, the most rapid stenographers, could not report the news it brings. No creature could move slowly where there was so much life around.

. . . . .

To-day it was the Purple Sea, an epithet which I should not before have accepted. There were distinct patches of the color of a purple grape with the bloom rubbed off. But first and last the sea is of all colors. Well writes Gilpin concerning "the brilliant hues which are continually playing on the surface of a quiet ocean," and this was not too turbulent at a distance from the shore.

"Beautiful," says he, "no doubt in a high degree are those glimmering tints which often invest the tops of mountains; but they are mere coruscations compared with these marine colors, which are continually varying and shifting into each other in all the vivid splendor of the rainbow, through the space often of several leagues."

Commonly, in calm weather, for half a mile from the shore, where the bottom tinges it, the sea is green, or greenish, as are some ponds; then blue for many miles, often with purple tinges,

73

bounded in the distance by a light, almost silvery stripe; beyond which there is generally a dark blue rim, like a mountain ridge in the horizon, as if, like that, it owed its color to the intervening atmosphere. On another day, it will be marked with long streaks, alternately smooth and rippled, light-colored and dark, even like our inland meadows in a freshet, and showing which way the wind sets. Thus we sat on the foaming shore, looking on the wine-colored ocean. . . .

Here and there was a darker spot on its surface, the shadow of a cloud, though the sky was so clear that no cloud would have been noticed otherwise, and no shadow would have been seen on the land, where a much smaller surface is visible at once. So, distant clouds and showers may be seen on all sides by a sailor in the course of a day, which do not necessarily portend rain where he is. In July we saw similar dark blue patches where schools of Menhaden rippled the surface, scarcely to be distinguished from the shadows of clouds. Sometimes the sea was spotted with them far and wide, such is its inexhaustible fertility. Close at hand you see their back fin, which is very long and sharp, projecting two or three inches above water. From time to time also we saw the white bellies of the Bass playing along the shore.

The Sea and The Cape

The action of the winds, rains, and waves is constantly changing the shape of Cape Cod. Of the original ten acres purchased by the government for the Highland Light, something less than four now remain. At the headwaters of the Pamet River in Truro, only a small dike of sand keeps the river from joining the salt meadows to the west. If the ocean broke through and established a channel, Provincetown and North Truro would find themselves an island. Billingsgate Island, which is now a small sand bar off Wellfleet Harbor, once had thirty houses, a school, and a lighthouse. The people there fished for a living, and also cultivated gardens. Today nothing remains of this community except an occasional remanent turned up in the sand by a visiting fisherman. On the other hand, the tides, winds, and waves have piled up sand against many of the shoals, which are now growing in size and may eventually become land.

The sea is not gaining on the Cape everywhere, for one man told me of a vessel wrecked long ago on the north of Provincetown whose *"bones"* (this was his word) are still visible many

75

rods within the present line of the beach, half buried in sand. Perchance they lie alongside the *timbers* of a whale. The general statement of the inhabitants is, that the Cape is wasting on both sides, but extending itself on particular points on the south and west, as at Chatham and Monomoy Beaches, and at Billingsgate, Long, and Race Points. James Freeman stated in his day that above three miles had been added to Monomoy Beach during the previous fifty years, and it is said to be still extending as fast as ever. A writer in the Massachusetts Magazine, in the last century, tells us that "when the English first settled upon the Cape, there was an island off Chatham, at three leagues' distance, called Webbs' Island, containing twenty acres, covered with red-cedar or savin. The inhabitants of Nantucket used to carry wood from it;" but he adds that in his day a large rock alone marked the spot, and the water was six fathoms deep there. The entrance to Nauset Harbor, which was once in Eastham, has now traveled south into Orleans. The islands in Wellfleet Harbor once formed a continuous beach, though now small vessels pass between them. And so of many other parts of this coast.

Perhaps what the Ocean takes from one part of the Cape it gives to another,—robs Peter to pay Paul. On the eastern side the sea appears to be everywhere encroaching on the land. Not only the land is undermined, and its ruins carried off by currents, but the sand is blown from the beach directly up the steep bank, where it is one hundred and fifty feet high, and covers the original surface there many feet deep. If you sit on the edge you will have ocular demonstration of this by soon getting your eyes full. Thus the bank preserves its height as fast as it is worn away. This sand is steadily traveling westward at a rapid rate, "more than a hundred yards," says one writer, within the memory of inhabitants now living; so that in some places peat-meadows are buried deep under the sand, and the peat is cut through it; and in one place a large peat-meadow has made its appearance on the shore in the bank covered many feet deep, and peat has been cut there. This accounts for that great pebble of peat which we saw in the surf.[1]

[1 Pieces of peat resembling rocks can still be seen occasionally along the beach.— A.B.A.]

⤐ Stone and Pebbles

The visitor to Cape Cod will be struck, as Thoreau was, by the absence of both stones and rocks. This is clearly apparent at Wellfleet Harbor when the tide is out. There are many shoals and reefs to endanger the boatsman, but hardly a rock or stone on the entire harbor bottom. At Eastham a large boulder known as Eastham's Great Rock will be found to the right of Doane Road, leading down to the Coast Guard Beach. It is considered such a feature that it is now surrounded by a town park. Generations of Easthamers have gathered near it for picnics and other important occasions.

⤐ We eagerly filled our pockets with the smooth round pebbles which in some places, even here, were thinly sprinkled over the sand, together with flat circular shells (*Scutellæ?*); but, as we had read, when they were dry they had lost their beauty, and at each sitting we emptied our pockets again of the least remarkable, until our collection was well culled. Every material was rolled into the pebble form by the waves; not only stones of various kinds, but the hard coal which some vessel had dropped, bits of glass, and in one instance a mass of peat three feet long, where there was nothing like it to be seen for many

79

miles. All the great rivers of the globe are annually, if not constantly, discharging great quantities of lumber, which drifts to distant shores.

I have also seen very perfect pebbles of brick, and bars of Castile soap from a wreck rolled into perfect cylinders, and still spirally streaked with red, like a barber's pole. When a cargo of rags is washed ashore, every old pocket and bag-like recess will be filled to bursting with sand by being rolled on the beach; and on one occasion, the pockets in the clothing of the wrecked thus being puffed up, even after they had been ripped open by wreckers, deluded me into the hope of identifying them by the contents. A pair of gloves looked exactly as if filled by a hand. The water in such clothing is soon wrung out and evaporated, but the sand, which works itself into every seam, is not so easily got rid of. Sponges, which are picked up on the shore, as is well known, retain some of the sand of the beach to the latest day, in spite of every effort to extract it.

I found one stone on the top of the bank, of a dark gray color, shaped exactly like a giant clam (*Mactra solidissima*), and of the same size; and, what was more remarkable, one half of the outside had shelled off and lay near it, of the same form and depth with one of the valves of this clam, while the other half was loose, leaving a solid core of a darker color within it. I afterward saw a stone resembling a razor clam, but it was a solid one. It appeared as if the stone, in the process of formation, had filled the mould which a clam-shell furnished; or the same law that shaped the clam had made a clam of stone. Dead clams, with shells full of sand, are called sand clams. There were many of the large clam-shells filled with sand; and sometimes one valve was separately filled exactly even, as if it had been heaped and then scraped. Even among the many small stones on the top of the bank, I found one arrow-head.

. . . . .

Stones are very rare on the Cape. I saw a very few small stones used for pavements and for bank walls, in one or two places in my walk, but they are so scarce, that, as I was informed, vessels have been forbidden to take them from the beach for ballast, and therefore their crews used to land at night and steal them. I did not hear of a rod of regular stone wall below Orleans. Yet I saw one man underpinning a new house in Eastham with some "rocks," as he called them, which he said a neighbor had collected with great pains in the course of years, and finally made over to him. This I thought was a gift worthy of being recorded, —equal to a transfer of California "rocks," almost. Another man who was assisting him, and who seemed to be a close observer of nature, hinted to me the locality of a rock in the neighborhood which was "forty-two paces in circumference and fifteen feet high," for he saw that I was a stranger, and, probably, would not carry it off. Yet I suspect that the locality of the few large rocks on the forearm of the Cape is well known to the inhabitants generally. I even met with one man who had got a smattering of mineralogy, but where he picked it up I could not guess. I thought that he would meet with some interesting geological nuts for him to crack, if he should ever visit the mainland,— Cohasset or Marblehead, for instance.

The well stones at the Highland Light were brought from Hingham, but the wells and cellars of the Cape are generally built of brick, which also are imported. The cellars, as well as the wells, are made in a circular form, to prevent the sand from pressing in the wall. The former are only from nine to twelve feet in diameter, and are said to be very cheap, since a single tier of brick will suffice for a cellar of even larger dimensions. Of course, if you live in the sand, you will not require a large cellar to hold your roots.

~ Stores from the Sea

Some idea of the supplies that the ocean once threw up on Cape Cod's shores can be gotten by looking at a few historical events. In the month of December 1839, twenty-one vessels were lost off Cape Cod. During a single storm in October 1841, the beach at Nauset was strewn with barrels, cabin furniture, and whole sections of ships. At one time or another almost every type of cargo has been wrecked off the shores of Cape Cod, ranging from coffee beans and cotton to $80,000 in specie, which was aboard the ship *Maine*, bound from Batavia to Boston. Today, however, the beachcomber is fortunate to find anything more than a supply of driftwood.

~   The objects around us, the makeshifts of fishermen ashore, often made us look down to see if we were standing on terra firma. In the wells everywhere a block and tackle were used to raise the bucket, instead of a windlass, and by almost every house was laid up a spar or a plank or two full of auger-holes, saved from a wreck. The windmills were partly built of these, and they were worked into the public bridges. The light-house keeper, who was having his barn shingled, told me casually that he had made three thousand good shingles for that purpose out of a mast. You would sometimes see an old oar used for a rail. Frequently also some fair-weather finery ripped off a vessel by a storm near the coast was nailed up against an outhouse. I saw fastened to a shed near the light-house a long new sign with the words "ANGLO SAXON" on it in large gilt letters, as if it were a useless part which the ship could afford to lose, or which the sailors had discharged at the same time with the pilot. But it interested somewhat as if it had been a part of the Argo, clipped off in passing through the Symplegades.

To the fisherman, the Cape itself is a sort of store-ship laden with supplies,—a safer and larger craft which carries the women and children, the old men and the sick, and indeed sea-phrases are as common on it as on board a vessel. Thus is it ever with a sea-going people. The old Northmen used to speak of the "keel-ridge" of the country, that is, the ridge of the Doffrafield Mountains, as if the land were a boat turned bottom up. I was frequently reminded of the Northmen here. The inhabitants of the Cape are often at once farmers and sea-rovers; they are more than vikings or kings of the bays, for their sway extends over the open sea also. A farmer in Wellfleet, at whose house I afterward spent a night, who had raised fifty bushels of potatoes the previous year, which is a large crop for the Cape, and had extensive salt-works, pointed to his schooner, which lay in sight, in which he and his man and boy occasionally ran down the coast a-trading as far as the Capes of Virginia. This was his market-cart, and his hired man knew how to steer her. Thus he drove two teams a-field.

> "ere the high *seas* appeared
> Under the opening eyelids of the morn."

Though probably he would not hear much of the "gray-fly" on his way to Virginia.

A great proportion of the inhabitants of the Cape are always thus abroad about their teaming on some ocean highway or other, and the history of one of their ordinary trips would cast the Argonautic expedition into the shade. I have just heard of a Cape Cod captain who was expected home in the beginning of the winter from the West Indies, but was long since given up for lost, till his relations at length have heard with joy, that after getting within forty miles of Cape Cod light,[1] he was driven back by nine successive gales to Key West, between Florida and Cuba, and was once again shaping his course for home. Thus he spent his winter. In ancient times the adventures of these two or three men and boys would have been made the basis of a myth, but now such tales are crowded into a line of shorthand signs, like an algebraic formula in the shipping news.

[1 The Highland Light.—A.B.A.]

Beach Grass

The formation of dunes is dependent on certain standard conditions, including strong, prevailing winds and a beach of sand that is continually being replenished from off-shore sand bars. As the wind sweeps across the beach, it picks up sand particles. When it loses its velocity farther inland by meeting an obstruction such as a tree line or a sand dune, it deposits part of its load. In this way, the process of build-up is started. After the dune has reached a certain size, it will generally creep in the direction the wind is going, for some sand will be deposited on the leeward side but, at the same time, some will be removed from windward. "Live" dunes, as they are called, can be stabilized by two principal methods. One is to construct snow fences, which tend to increase the build-up, and the other is to plant grasses, whose roots will hold the loose sands in place. Such grasses are highly specialized, because living conditions in the dunes are severe. The grass must be able to protect itself from being buried by fresh sand brought in by the wind, from sudden changes in temperature, and also from a high degree of salinity. In writing about beach grass, Thoreau has not exaggerated its importance to Cape Cod. The loss of beach grass on the Cape would be a major disaster.

In Dwight's Travels in New England it is stated that the inhabitants of Truro were formerly regularly warned under the authority of law in the month of April yearly, to plant beach-grass, as elsewhere they are warned to repair the highways. They dug up the grass in bunches, which were afterward divided into several smaller ones, and set about three feet apart, in rows, so arranged as to break joints and obstruct the passage of the wind. It spread itself rapidly, the weight of the seeds when ripe bending the heads of the grass, and so dropping directly by its side and vegetating there. In this way, for instance, they built up again that part of the Cape between Truro and Provincetown where the sea broke over in the last century. They have now a public road near there, made by laying sods, which were full of roots, bottom upward and close together on the sand, double in the middle of the track, then spreading brush evenly over the sand on each side for half a dozen feet, planting beach-grass on the banks in regular rows, as above described, and sticking a fence of brush against the hollows.

The attention of the general government was first attracted to the danger which threatened Cape Cod Harbor[1] from the inroads of the sand, about thirty years ago, and commissioners were at the time appointed by Massachusetts to examine the premises. They reported in June, 1825, that, owing to "the trees and brush having been cut down, and the beach-grass destroyed on the seaward side of the Cape, opposite the Harbor," the original surface of the ground had been broken up and removed by the wind toward the Harbor,—during the previous fourteen years,—over an extent of "one half a mile in breadth, and about four and a half miles in length."—"The space where a few years since were some of the highest lands on the Cape, covered with trees and bushes," presenting "an extensive waste of undulating sand;"—and that, during the previous twelve months, the sand

[1On many old charts, Cape Cod Harbor is used as the name for Provincetown Harbor.]

"had approached the Harbor an average distance of fifty rods, for an extent of four and a half miles!" and unless some measures were adopted to check its progress, it would in a few years destroy both the harbor and the town. They therefore recommended that beach-grass be set out on a curving line over a space ten rods wide and four and a half miles long, and that cattle, horses, and sheep be prohibited from going abroad, and the inhabitants from cutting the bush.

. . . . .

Thus Cape Cod is anchored to the heavens, as it were, by a myriad little cables of beach-grass, and, if they should fail, would become a total wreck, and erelong go to the bottom.

⋖ Old Anchors

The simplest and most direct way to lose an anchor is to drop it overboard without tying down the line that should connect it to the boat. Improbable as it may seem, this has been done numerous times by inexperienced sailors in the excitement of coming to anchor. Or sometimes the anchor becomes jammed and cannot be raised; or the hawser breaks; or the anchor has been left in place and marked with a buoy that has subsequently torn free. Because there is little depreciation in value, anchors make worthwhile salvage. They can be put to work again on a ship or, as is still done on Cape Cod, be used for decoration.

⋖ [One] summer I saw a sloop from Chatham dragging for anchors and chains just off this shore. She had her boats out at the work while she shuffled about on various tacks, and, when anything was found, drew up to hoist it on board. It is a singular employment, at which men are regularly hired and paid for their industry, to hunt to-day in pleasant weather for anchors which have been lost,—the sunken faith and hope of mariners, to which they trusted in vain; now, perchance, it is the rusty one of some old pirate's ship or Norman fisherman, whose cable parted here two hundred years ago, and now the best bower anchor of a Canton or a California ship, which has gone about her business.

If the roadsteads of the spiritual ocean could be thus dragged, what rusty flukes of hope deceived and parted chain-cables of faith might again be windlassed aboard! enough to sink the finder's craft, or stock new navies to the end of time. The bottom of the sea is strewn with anchors, some deeper and some shallower, and alternately covered and uncovered by the sand, perchance with a small length of iron cable still attached,—to which where is the other end? So many unconcluded tales to be continued another time. So, if we had diving-bells adapted to the spiritual deeps, we should see anchors with their cables attached, as thick as eels in vinegar, all wriggling vainly toward their holding-ground. But that is not treasure for us which another man has lost; rather it is for us to seek what no other man has found or can find,—not be Chatham men, dragging for anchors.

The Wrist of the Cape

By looking at an overall map of the Cape, the visitor can immediately see what Thoreau means by the "wrist." It is the area between North Truro and Provincetown, where the Cape becomes narrow and slender before turning into the "fist" at its extremity. While continuing on Route 6 toward Provincetown, the visitor will find several side trips worth while. One of these will take him to the right just before reaching Pilgrim Lake, which he cannot miss because it is the largest lake he will see on this trip. The road is known as High Head Road and leads to the beach. Pilgrim Heights is the bluff on the eastern end of Pilgrim Lake. The view from the top makes the trip up well worth the time. By this point the signs warning the motorist not to stop on the shoulders of roads become more and more common and, to the initiated, more and more meaningful.

The Cape became narrower and narrower as we approached its wrist between Truro and Provincetown and the shore inclined more decidedly to the west. At the head of East Harbor[1] Creek, the Atlantic is separated but by half a dozen rods of sand from the tide-waters of the Bay. From the

[1 Pilgrim Lake was once open to the sea and known as East Harbor.—A.B.A.]

93

Clay Pounds the bank flatted off for the last ten miles to the extremity at Race Point, though the highest parts, which are called "islands" from their appearance at a distance on the sea, were still seventy or eighty feet above the Atlantic, and afforded a good view of the latter, as well as a constant view of the Bay, there being no trees nor a hill sufficient to interrupt it. Also the sands began to invade the land more and more, until finally they had entire possession from sea to sea, at the narrowest part. For three or four miles between Truro and Provincetown there were no inhabitants from shore to shore, and there were but three or four houses for twice that distance.

As we plodded along, either by the edge of the ocean, where the sand was rapidly drinking up the last wave that wet it, or over the sandhills of the bank, the mackerel fleet continued to pour round the Cape north of us, ten or fifteen miles distant, in countless numbers, schooner after schooner, till they made a city on the water. They were so thick that many appeared to be afoul of one another; now all standing on this tack, now on that. We saw how well the New-Englanders had followed up Captain John Smith's suggestions with regard to the fisheries, made in 1616,—to what a pitch they had carried "this contemptible trade of fish," as he significantly styles it, and were now equal to the Hollanders whose example he holds up for the English to emulate; notwithstanding that "in this faculty," as he says, "the former are so naturalized, and of their vents so certainly acquainted, as there is no likelihood they will ever be paralleled, having two or three thousand busses, flat-bottoms, sword-pinks, todes, and such like, that breeds them sailors, mariners, soldier, and merchants, never to be wrought out of that trade and fit for any other."

We thought that it would take all these names and more to describe the numerous craft which we saw.

. . . . .

. . . The gazetteer tells you gravely how many of the men and boys of these towns are engaged in the whale, cod, and mackerel fishery, how many go to the banks of Newfoundland, or the coast of Labrador, the Straits of Belle Isle or the Bay of Chaleurs—Shalore, the sailors call it; as if I were to reckon up the number of boys in Concord who are engaged during the summer in the perch, pickerel, bream, horn-pout, and shiner fishery, of which no one keeps the statistics,—though I think that it is pursued with as much profit to the moral and intellectual man (or boy), and certainly with less danger to the physical one.

⋘ Mount Ararat

At the western end of Pilgrim Lake—the end nearest Provincetown—is a tight clump of dunes known as Mount Ararat. They are approximately a hundred feet high and can be identified by the sand quarry at their base. The slopes of sand are tempting to the hiker today, just as they were tempting to Thoreau. But walking over sands can be hot, tiring work; and unrestricted hiking tends to destroy the dunes by changing their surfaces and damaging the grasses that help hold them together.

⋘ Having passed the narrowest part of the waist of the Cape, though still in Truro, for this township is about twelve miles long on the shore, we crossed over to the Bay side, not half a mile distant, in order to spend the noon on the nearest shrubby sand-hill in Provincetown, called Mount Ararat, which rises one hundred feet above the ocean. On our way thither we had occasion to admire the various beautiful forms and colors of the sand, and we noticed an interesting mirage, which I have since found that Hitchcock also observed on the sands of the Cape.

97

We were crossing a shallow valley in the desert, where the smooth and spotless sand sloped upward by a small angle to the horizon on every side, and at the lowest part was a long chain of clear but shallow pools. As we were approaching these for a drink, in a diagonal direction across the valley, they appeared inclined at a slight but decided angle to the horizon, though they were plainly and broadly connected with one another, and there was not the least ripple to suggest a current; so that by the time we had reached a convenient part of one we seemed to have ascended several feet. They appeared to lie by magic on the side of the vale, like a mirror left in a slanting position. It was a very pretty mirage for a Provincetown desert, but not amounting to what, in Sanscrit, is called "the thirst of the gazelle," as there was real water here for a base, and we were able to quench our thirst after all.

· · · · ·

From the above-mentioned sand-hill we overlooked Provincetown and its harbor, now emptied of vessels, and also a wide expanse of ocean. As we did not wish to enter Provincetown before night, though it was cold and windy, we returned across the deserts to the Atlantic side, and walked along the beach again nearly to Race Point, being still greedy of the sea influence. All the while it was not so calm as the reader may suppose, but it was blow, blow, blow,—roar, roar, roar,—tramp, tramp, tramp,—without interruption. The shore now trended nearly east and west.

⤙ Provincetown

Above all, the visitor to Provincetown must remember that the Pilgrims did *not* land first at Plymouth, which is an upstart to citizens of Provincetown. It was here that the Pilgrims first touched the soil of the New World, on November 11, 1620. The *Mayflower* remained at anchor in the harbor for almost two months until it proceeded to Plymouth. Four members of the Pilgrims' group died here, and the first child to be born in New England of English parents was born in Provincetown. The Mayflower Compact, which contained the Pilgrims' articles of self-government, was written in the cabin of the *Mayflower* as it lay anchored in Provincetown Harbor. This covenant is considered one of the most important documents historically in the development of American government. Once an important fishing and shipping center, Provincetown has also become famous as a writers' and artists' colony. Eugene O'Neill is among the many noted writers who have lived here.

⤙ This was the most completely maritime town that we were ever in. It was merely a good harbor, surrounded by land,

99

dry if not firm,—an inhabited beach, whereon fishermen cured and stored their fish, without any back country. When ashore the inhabitants still walk on planks. A few small patches have been reclaimed from the swamps, containing commonly half a dozen square rods only each. We saw one which was fenced with four lengths of rail; also a fence made wholly of hogshead staves stuck in the ground. These, and such as these, were all the cultivated and cultivable land in Provincetown. We were told that there were thirty or forty acres in all, but we did not discover a quarter part so much, and that was well dusted with sand, and looked as if the desert was claiming it. They are now turning some of their swamps into Cranberry Meadows on quite an extensive scale.

Yet far from being out of the way, Provincetown is directly in the way of the navigator, and he is lucky who does not run afoul of it in the dark. It is situated on one of the highways of commerce, and men from all parts of the globe touch there in the course of a year.

. . . . .

The Harbor of Provincetown—which, as well as the greater part of the Bay, and a wide expanse of ocean, we overlooked from our perch—is deservedly famous. It opens to the south, is free from rocks, and is never frozen over. It is said that the only ice seen in it drifts in sometimes from Barnstable or Plymouth. Dwight remarks that "the storms which prevail on the American coast generally come from the east; and there is no other harbor on a windward shore within two hundred miles." J. D. Graham, who has made a very minute and thorough survey of this harbor and the adjacent waters, states that "its capacity, depth of water, excellent anchorage, and the complete shelter it affords from all winds, combine to render it one of the most valuable ship harbors on our coast."

It is *the* harbor of the Cape and of the fishermen of Massachusetts generally. It was known to navigators several years at least before the settlement of Plymouth. In Captain John

Smith's map of New England, dated 1614, it bears the name of Milford Haven, and Massachusetts Bay that of Stuard's Bay. His Highness Prince Charles changed the name of Cape Cod to Cape James; but even princes have not always power to change a name for the worse, and, as Cotton Mather said, Cape Cod is "a name which I suppose it will never lose till shoals of codfish be seen swimming on its highest hills."

Many an early traveler was unexpectedly caught by this hook, and found himself embayed.

. . . . .

The sand is the great enemy here. The tops of some of the hills were inclosed and a board put up forbidding all persons entering the inclosure, lest their feet should disturb the sand, and set it a-blowing or a-sliding. The inhabitants are obliged to get leave from the authorities to cut wood behind the town for fish-flakes, bean-poles, pea-brush, and the like, though, as we were told, they may transplant trees from one part of the township to another without leave. The sand drifts like snow, and sometimes the lower story of a house is concealed by it, though it is kept off by a wall. The houses were formerly built on piles, in order that the driving sand might pass under them. We saw a few old ones here still standing on their piles, but they were boarded up now, being protected by their younger neighbors.

There was a school-house, just under the hill on which we sat, filled with sand up to the tops of the desks, and of course the master and scholars had fled. Perhaps they had imprudently left the windows open one day, or neglected to mend a broken pane. Yet in one place was advertised "Fine sand for sale here,"—I could hardly believe my eyes,—probably some of the street sifted,—a good instance of the fact that a man confers a value on the most worthless thing by mixing himself with it, according to which rule we must have conferred a value on the whole back-side of Cape Cod;—but I thought that if they could have advertised "Fat Soil," or perhaps "Fine sand got rid of," ay, and "Shoes emptied here," it would have been more alluring.

As we looked down on the town, I thought that I saw one man, who probably lived beyond the extremity of the planking, steering and tacking for it in a sort of snow-shoes, but I may have been mistaken. In some pictures of Provincetown the persons of the inhabitants are not drawn below the ankles, so much being supposed to be buried in the sand. Nevertheless, natives of Provincetown assured me that they could walk in the middle of the road without trouble even in slippers, for they had learned how to put their feet down and lift them up without taking in any sand. One man said that he should be surprised if he found half a dozen grains of sand in his pumps at night, and stated, moreover, that the young ladies had a dexterous way of emptying their shoes at each step, which it would take a stranger a long time to learn.

Boys of Provincetown

Although the fishing industry is no longer as important as it once was at Provincetown, the municipal wharves are still a center of interest and well worth the visitor's time. The town's small boys continue to gather there. They may eventually make their living at any one of hundreds of businesses, but they cannot live at Provincetown without the sea's getting into their blood. Many of them are not descendants of original settlers, and the visitor will be surprised at the numbers of Portuguese names that he will encounter. The Portuguese came to Provincetown during whaling days from the Azores, the Canaries, the Cape Verde Islands, and Portugal proper. They have been here so long they are now true Cape Codders.

After making an excursion among the hills in the neighborhood of the Shank-Painter Swamp,[1] and getting a little work done in its line, we took our seat upon the highest sand-hill overlooking the town, in mid-air, on a long plank stretched across between two hillocks of sand, where some boys were

[1 Shank-Painter Swamp is on the left-hand side of Route 6 just before it reaches Provincetown Beach.—A.B.A.]

103

endeavoring in vain to fly their kite; and there we remained the rest of that forenoon looking out over the placid harbor, and watching for the first appearance of the steamer from Wellfleet, that we might be in readiness to go on board when we heard the whistle off Long Point.

We got what we could out of the boys in the mean while. Provincetown boys are of course all sailors and have sailors' eyes. When we were at the Highland Light the last summer, seven or eight miles from Provincetown Harbor, and wished to know one Sunday morning if the Olata, a well-known yacht, had got in from Boston, so that we could return in her, a Provincetown boy about ten years old, who chanced to be at the table, remarked that she had. I asked him how he knew. "I just saw her come in," said he. When I expressed surprise that he could distinguish her from other vessels so far, he said that there were not so many of those two-topsail schooners about but that he could tell her. Palfrey[2] said, in his oration at Barnstable, the duck does not take to the water with a surer instinct than the Barnstable boy. (He might have said the Cape Cod boy as well.) He leaps from his leading-strings into the shrouds, it is but a bound from the mother's lap to the masthead. He boxes the compass in his infant soliloquies. He can hand, reef, and steer by the time he flies a kite.

[2 A Unitarian minister from Boston who edited *The North American Review* and wrote a history of New England.—A.B.A.]

East of
Provincetown

Although Provincetown is a cosmopolitan town and **a** center for tourists, the areas east and north of the town are still relatively wild and unspoiled. They are dotted with hummocks, ponds, marshes, and beaches. A few roads lead through this part of the Cape, but it can best be reached by walking. A good starting place is Provincetown Beach at the end of Route 6.

. . . we left the seashore on the north of Provincetown, and made our way across the desert to the eastern extremity of the town. From the first high sand-hill, covered with beach-grass and bushes to its top, on the edge of the desert, we overlooked the shrubby hill and swamp country which surrounds Provincetown on the north, and protects it, in some measure, from the invading sand. Notwithstanding the universal barrenness, and the contiguity of the desert, I never saw an autumnal landscape so beautifully painted as this was.

It was like the richest rug imaginable spread over an uneven surface; no damask nor velvet, nor Tyrian dye or stuffs, nor the work of any loom, could ever match it. There was the incredibly bright red of the Huckleberry, and the reddish brown of the Bayberry, mingled with the bright and living green of small Pitch-Pines, and also the duller green of the Bayberry, Boxberry, and Plum, the yellowish green of the Shrub-Oaks, and the various golden and yellow and fawn-colored tints of the Birch and Maple and Aspen,—each making its own figure, and, in the midst, the few yellow sandslides on the sides of the hills looked like the white floor seen through rents in the rug.

Coming from the country as I did, and many autumnal woods as I had seen, this was perhaps the most novel and remarkable sight that I saw on the Cape. Probably the brightness of the tints was enhanced by contrast with the sand which surrounded this tract. This was a part of the furniture of Cape Cod. We had for days walked up the long and bleak piazza which runs along her Atlantic side, then over the sanded floor of her halls, and now we were being introduced into her boudoir. The hundred white sails crowding round Long Point[1] into Provincetown Harbor, seen over the painted hills in front, looked like toy ships upon a mantel-piece.

The peculiarity of this autumnal landscape consisted in the lowness and thickness of the shrubbery, no less than in the brightness of the tints. It was like a thick stuff of worsted or a fleece, and looked as if a giant could take it up by the hem, or rather the tasseled fringe which trailed out on the sand, and shake it, though it needed not to be shaken. But no doubt the dust would fly in that case, for not a little has accumulated underneath it. Was it not such an autumnal landscape as this which suggested our high-colored rugs and carpets? Hereafter when I look on a richer rug than usual, and study its figures, I shall think, there are the huckleberry hills, and there the denser swamps of boxberry and blueberry; there the shrub-oak patches and the bayberries, there the maples and the birches and the pines. What other dyes are to be compared to these?

[1 The point that hooks around to make Provincetown Harbor.—A.B.A.]

⬷ Race Point

Race Point Road leads north from Route 6 in back of Provincetown and runs to the Race Point Coast Guard Station. On the way, the visitor will pass a small elevated platform that serves as a lookout. This is worth visiting. In spite of its apparently small height, it offers a good view of the area. A little farther on toward his left, the visitor will see the Provincetown Airport, where airborne sight-seeing trips can be arranged. At the beach near the Race Point Coast Guard Station, rides in "beach buggies" are offered. These are cars with oversized tires that can drive across the beaches and dunes. While many old-time Cape Codders are scornful of such tourist attractions, a ride in a beach buggy is a quick and easy way to see what the dunes and beaches are like.

⬷ The next morning, though it was still more cold and blustering than the day before, we took to the deserts again, for we spent our days wholly out of doors, in the sun when there was any, and in the wind which never failed. After threading the shrubby hill-country at the southwest end of the town, west of the Shank-Painter Swamp, whose expressive name—

for we understood it at first as a landsman naturally would—gave it importance in our eyes, we crossed the sands to the shore south of Race Point and three miles distant, and thence roamed round eastward through the desert to where we had left the sea the evening before. We traveled five or six miles after we got out there, on a curving line, and might have gone nine or ten, over vast platters of pure sand, from the midst of which we could not see a particle of vegetation, excepting the distant thin fields of beach-grass, which crowned and made the ridges toward which the sand sloped upward on each side; —all the while in the face of a cutting wind as cold as January; indeed, we experienced no weather so cold as this for nearly two months afterward.

This desert extends from the extremity of the Cape, through Provincetown into Truro, and many a time as we were traversing it we were reminded of "Riley's Narrative" of his captivity in the sands of Arabia, notwithstanding the cold. Our eyes magnified the patches of beach-grass into cornfields, in the horizon, and we probably exaggerated the height of the ridges on account of the mirage.

· · · · ·

The beach-grass is "two to four feet high, of a sea-green color," and it is said to be widely diffused over the world. In the Hebrides it is used for mats, pack-saddles, bags, hats, etc.; paper has been made of it at Dorchester in this State, and cattle eat it when tender. It has heads somewhat like rye, from six inches to a foot in length, and it is propagated both by roots and seeds. To express its love for sand, some botanists have called it *Psamma arenaria,* which is the Greek for sand, qualified by the Latin for sandy,—or sandy sand. As it is blown about by the wind, while it is held fast by its roots, it describes myriad circles in the sand as accurately as if they were made by compasses.

It was the dreariest scenery imaginable. The only animals which we saw on the sand at that time were spiders, which are

108

to be found almost everywhere whether on snow or ice, water or sand,—and a venomous-looking, long, narrow worm, one of the myriapods, or thousand-legs. We were surprised to see spider-holes in that flowing sand with an edge as firm as that of a stoned well.

In June this sand was scored with the tracks of turtles both large and small, which had been out in the night, leading to and from the swamps. I was told by a *terræ filius* who has a "farm" on the edge of the desert, and is familiar with the fame of Provincetown, that one man had caught twenty-five snapping-turtles there the previous spring. His own method of catching them was to put a toad on a mackerel-hook and cast it into a pond, tying the line to a stump or stake on shore. Invariably the turtle when hooked crawled up the line to the stump, and was found waiting there by his captor, however long afterward. He also said that minks, muskrats, foxes, coons, and wild mice were found there, but no squirrels.

We heard of sea-turtles as large as a barrel being found on the beach and on East Harbor marsh, but whether they were native there, or had been lost out of some vessel, did not appear. Perhaps they were the Salt-water Terrapin, or else the Smooth Terrapin, found thus far north. Many toads were met with where there was nothing but sand and beach-grass. In Truro I had been surprised at the number of large light-colored toads everywhere hopping over the dry and sandy fields, their color corresponding to that of the sand. Snakes also are common on these pure sand beaches, and I have never been so much troubled by mosquitoes as in such localities. At the same season strawberries grew there abundantly in the little hollows on the edge of the desert, standing amid the beach-grass in the sand, and the fruit of the shad-bush or *Amelanchier,* which the inhabitants call Josh-pears (some think from juicy?), is very abundant on the hills.

◄ The Back-Side

While the Back-side refers generally to the ocean as opposed to the Bay side of the Lower Cape, Thoreau is here referring to the Back-side north of Provincetown. Its exposed position makes it a particularly wild spot on a windy day. If the wind and tide are right, the visitor can see water breaking over the offshore bars that are so dangerous to shipping.

◄ We saw nobody that day outside of the town; it was too wintry for such as had seen the Back-side before, or for the greater number who never desire to see it, to venture out; and we saw hardly a track to show that any had ever crossed this desert. Yet I was told that some are always out on the Back-side night and day in severe weather, looking for wrecks, in order that they may get the job of discharging the cargo, or the like,—and thus shipwrecked men are succored. But, generally speaking, the inhabitants rarely visit these sands. One who had lived in Provincetown thirty years told me that he had not been through to the north side within that time. Sometimes the natives themselves come near perishing by losing their way in snow-storms behind the town.

The wind was not a Sirocco or Simoon, such as we associate with the desert, but a New England northeaster,—and we sought shelter in vain under the sand-hills, for it blew all about them, rounding them into cones, and was sure to find us out on whichever side we sat. From time to time we lay down and drank at little pools in the sand, filled with pure, fresh water, all that was left, probably, of a pond or swamp. The air was filled with dust like snow, and cutting sand which made the face tingle, and we saw what it must be to face it when the weather was drier, and, if possible, windier still,—to face a migrating sand-bar in the air, which has picked up its duds and is off,—to be whipped with a cat, not o' nine-tails, but of a myriad of tails, and each one a sting to it. A Mr. Whitman, a former minister of Wellfleet, used to write to his inland friends that the blowing sand scratched the windows so that he was obliged to have one new pane set every week, that he might see out.

⚮ Cape Cod People

Most Cape Codders, like most other New Englanders, are an honest, down-to-earth sort of people with a wry sense of humor and a pride in their own history. Also like other New Englanders, they are extremely friendly and are taciturn only if they are being pushed too quickly. Many of them have also become a bit weary of being regarded as picturesque. The story is told about the Boston woman who exclaimed to a Cape Codder that there were so many quaint people around. He immediately agreed with her but added, "Most of them leave right after Labor Day." The visitor who is truly interested in Cape Cod will find the people helpful and responsive, but he is warned not to ask foolish or obvious questions if he wants to avoid biting responses.

⚮ . . . So we took leave of Cape Cod and its inhabitants. We liked the manners of the last, what little we saw of them, very much. They were particularly downright and good-humored. The old people appeared remarkably well preserved, as if by the saltness of the atmosphere, and after having once mistaken, we could never be certain whether we were talking

113

to a coeval of our grandparents, or to one of our own age. They are said to be more purely the descendants of the Pilgrims than the inhabitants of any other part of the State. We were told that "sometimes, when the court comes together at Barnstable, they have not a single criminal to try, and the jail is shut up." It was "to let" when we were there. Until quite recently there was no regular lawyer below Orleans. Who then will complain of a few regular man-eating sharks along the Backside?

One of the ministers of Truro, when I asked what the fishermen did in the winter, answered that they did nothing but go a-visiting, sit about and tell stories,—though they worked hard in summer. Yet it is not a long vacation they get. I am sorry that I have not been there in the winter to hear their yarns. Almost every Cape man is Captain of some craft or other,—every man at least who is at the head of his own affairs, though it is not every one that is, for some heads have the force of *Alpha privative*, negativing all the efforts which Nature would fain make through them. The greater number of men are merely corporals. It is worth the while to talk with one whom his neighbors address as Captain, though his craft may have long been sunk, and he may be holding by his teeth to the shattered mast of a pipe alone, and only gets half-seas-over in a figurative sense, now. He is pretty sure to vindicate his right to the title at last,—can tell one or two good stories at least.

⇐ To See the Ocean

There is only one way for the visitor to return from Provincetown: on Route 6, the way he got there, at least as far as Orleans. There he has a choice of routes depending on whether he wants to go down the center of the Cape or down either of its two shorelines. But at Provincetown he can, as Thoreau says, "stand there and put all America behind him."

⇐ We went to see the Ocean, and that is probably the best place of all our coast to go to. If you go by water, you may experience what it is to leave and to approach these shores; you may see the Stormy Petrel by the way, . . . running over the sea, and if the weather is but a little thick, may lose sight of the land in mid-passage. I do not know where there is another beach in the Atlantic States, attached to the mainland, so long, and at the same time so straight, and completely uninterrupted by creeks or coves or fresh-water rivers or marshes; for though there may be clear places on the map, they would probably be found by the foot traveler to be intersected by creeks and marshes; certainly there is none where there is a double way, such as I have described, a beach and a bank, which at the same time shows you the land and the sea, and part of the time two seas.

．　．　．　．　．

The time must come when this coast will be a place of resort for those New-Englanders who really wish to visit the seaside. At present it is wholly unknown to the fashionable world, and probably it will never be agreeable to them. If it is merely a ten-pin alley, or a circular railway, or an ocean of mint-julep, that the visitor is in search of,—if he thinks more of the wine than the brine, as I suspect some do at Newport,—I trust that for a long time he will be disappointed here.

But this shore will never be more attractive than it is now. Such beaches as are fashionable are here made and unmade in a day, I may almost say, by the sea shifting its sands. Lynn and Nantasket! this bare and bended arm it is that makes the bay in which they lie so snugly. What are springs and waterfalls? Here is the spring of springs, the waterfall of waterfalls. A storm in the fall or winter is the time to visit it; a light-house or a fisherman's hut the true hotel. A man may stand there and put all America behind him.

"The barren aspect of the land would hardly
be believed if described."   *(page 3)*

"They looked loose and slightly locomotive, like huge wounded birds, trailing a wing or a leg. . . ." (*page* 9)

"The great number of windows in the ends of the houses, and their irregularity in size and position, . . . struck us agreeably. . . ." (*page 12*)

"Men and boys would have appeared alike at a little distance, there being no object by which to measure them." (*page 14*)

"It is a wild, rank place, and there is no flattery in it." (*page 18*)

"The waves forever rolling to the land are too far-traveled and untamable to be familiar."
(*page 18*)

". . . the ocean is land-lord as well as sea-lord, and comes ashore without a wharf for the landing. . . ." (*page 21*)

"Objects on the beach, whether men or inanimate things, look not only exceedingly grotesque, but much larger and more wonderful than they actually are." *(page 24)*

"There was but little weed cast up here, . . . there being scarcely a rock for rock-weed to adhere to." (*page 27*)

"Some times we sat on the wet beach and watched the beach birds, sand-pipers and others, trotting along close to each wave, and waiting for the sea to cast up their breakfast." (*page 33*)

"I was told that probably a quarter of the fuel and a considerable part of the lumber used in North Truro was drift-wood. Many get *all* their fuel from the beach." (*page 39*)

"The trees were, if possible, rarer than the houses, excepting apple-trees. . . ." (*page 37*)

"Everything told of the sea, even when we did not see its waste or hear its roar." (*page 37*)

". . . a house was rarely visible
. . . and the solitude was that of
the ocean and the desert combined." (*page 43*)

"[Pamet River] rises in a hollow within a few rods of the Atlantic, and one who lives near its source told us that in high tides the sea leaked through. . . ." (*page 51*)

"Even this vast clay bank is fast wearing away." (*page 56*)

". . . in gales . . . you must hold
on to the light-house to prevent being blown into the Atlantic."
(*page* 59)

"Each wave left the sand all braided or woven. . . ." (*page 72*)

"Stones . . . are so scarce, that, as
I was informed, vessels have been
forbidden to take them from the
beach for ballast, and therefore
their crews used to land at night
and steal them." (*page 81*)

"The objects around us, the makeshifts of fishermen ashore, often
made us look down to see if we
were standing on terra firma."
(*page 83*)

"Thus Cape Cod is anchored to the heavens
. . . by a myriad little cables of beach-grass.
. . ." (page 89)

". . . the sand was rapidly drinking up the last wave that wet it.
. . ." (*page 94*)

"... the sands began to invade
the land more and more. . . ."
(page 94)

"On our way thither we had occasion to admire the various beautiful forms and colors of the sand. . . ." (*page* 97)

"It is *the* harbor of the Cape and of the fishermen of Massachusetts generally." (*page 100*)

"He leaps from his leading-strings into the shrouds, it is but a bound from the mother's lap to the mast-head." (*page 104*)

". . . we took to the deserts again,
for we spent our days wholly out
of doors. . . ." (*page 107*)

"It was the dreariest scenery imaginable."   (*page 108*)

"This desert extends from the extremity of the Cape, through Provincetown into Truro. . . ." (*page 108*)

"They are said to be more purely the descendants of the Pilgrims than the inhabitants of any
other part of the State."   (*page 114*)

". . . a beach and a bank. . . ." (*page 116*)

"I do not know where there is another beach in the Atlantic States, attached to the mainland, so long, and at the same time so straight. . . ."
(*page 115*)

⟨ Checklist of Points of Interest

The area of Cape Cod covered by this book includes what is known as the Lower Cape. The following is a partial list of points of interest arranged by towns.

EASTHAM

Old Windmill, just opposite the town hall.
Nauset Coast Guard Beach, which has excellent surf bathing.
Boulder on Doane Road, which is reputed to be the largest rock on Cape Cod.
First Encounter Beach, where the Pilgrims first met up with the Indians. Excellent swimming when the water is too rough at the Nauset Coast Guard Beach.
Nauset Light.

WELLFLEET

The town pier. Fishing boats can be rented here.
Site chosen by Marconi for the first wireless station in America to send messages overseas.
Historical Society on Main Street.

TRURO

Highland Light, the first American light to be seen by ships coming to Boston from Europe.

Corn Hill, where the Pilgrims dug up Indian corn in 1620.

Pilgrim Springs, where the Pilgrims obtained their first fresh water.

There are also a number of interesting old churchyards in Truro and North Truro.

PROVINCETOWN

Pilgrim Monument, a tall masonry tower dedicated in 1910. On a clear day the visitor can see almost the entire Cape from the top.

Provincetown Playhouse near the town hall. Some of Eugene O'Neill's first plays were produced here.

Chrysler Art Museum on Commercial Street.

Historical Museum on Commercial Street.

Observation Tower on the road to Race Point.

Fish wharves and town piers.

Early History of Cape Cod

No one knows who first discovered Cape Cod. It is highly probable that it was familiar to the Norsemen and to the Dutch and French fishermen who fished off the coast of Labrador. In 1602 the English navigator Bartholomew Gosnold anchored near Provincetown and gave the Cape its name. In 1603 Martin Pring arrived on a short expedition; he was followed in 1605 by Champlain, who returned again in 1606. Captain John Smith also explored the Cape. As noted earlier; one of his men, Captain Thomas Hunt, kidnapped several Indians to sell into slavery, and the incident created problems for the Pilgrims when they arrived in 1620 for their two-month layover at Provincetown.

From then until 1637 the Cape was visited mostly by fishermen, trappers, hunters, and traders. In 1637 Sandwich was founded, followed by Yarmouth, Barnstable, and Eastham. The other Cape towns were eventually carved out of these original four.

A Biographical Sketch of Thoreau

BY RALPH WALDO EMERSON

Emerson, one of America's eminent writers, was a neighbor of Thoreau's in Concord and a long-time friend and patron. He was born in 1803 and died in 1882. He wrote this sketch originally as an address to be used at Thoreau's funeral and later enlarged it. The following version is taken from the ten-volume, Riverside Edition of *The Writings of Henry David Thoreau*, published in 1896 by Houghton, Mifflin and Company, Boston.

Henry David Thoreau was the last male descendant of a French ancestor who came to this country from the Isle of Guernsey. His character exhibited occasional traits drawn from this blood in singular combination with a very strong Saxon genius.

He was born in Concord, Massachusetts, on the 12th of July, 1817. He was graduated at Harvard College in 1837, but without any literary distinction. An iconoclast in literature, he seldom thanked colleges for their service to him, holding them in small esteem, whilst yet his debt to them was important. After leaving the University, he joined his brother in teaching a private school, which he soon renounced. His father was a manufacturer of lead-pencils, and Henry applied himself for a time to this craft, believing he could make a better pencil than was then in use. After completing his experiments, he exhibited his work to chemists and artists in Boston, and having obtained their certificates to its excellence and to its equality with the best London manufacture, he returned home contented. His friends congratulated him that he had now opened his way to fortune. But he replied, that he should never make another pencil. "Why should I? I would not do again what I have done once." He resumed his endless walks and miscellaneous studies, making every day some new acquaintance with Nature, though as yet never speaking of zoology or botany, since, though very studious of natural facts, he was incurious of technical and textual science.

At this time, a strong, healthy youth, fresh from college, whilst all his companions were choosing their profession, or eager to begin some lucrative employment, it was inevitable that his thoughts should be exercised on the same question, and it required rare decision to refuse all the accustomed paths, and keep his solitary freedom at the cost of disappointing the natural expectations of his family and friends: all the more difficult that he had a perfect probity, was exact in securing his own independence, and in holding every man to the like duty. But Thoreau never faltered. He was a born protestant. He declined to give up his large ambition of knowledge and action for any narrow craft or profession, aiming at a much more comprehensive calling, the art of living well. If he slighted and defied the opinions of others, it was only that he was more intent to reconcile his practice with his own belief. Never idle or self-indulgent, he preferred, when he wanted money, earning it by some piece of manual labor agreeable to him, as building a boat or a fence, planting, grafting, surveying, or other short work, to any long engagements. With his hardy habits and few wants, his skill in wood-craft, and his powerful arithmetic, he was very competent to live in any part of the world. It would cost him less time to supply his wants than another. He was therefore secure of his leisure.

A natural skill for mensuration, growing out of his mathematical knowledge, and his habit of ascertaining the measures and distances of objects which interested him, the size of trees, the depth and extent of ponds and rivers, the height of mountains, and air-line distance of his favorite summits,—this, and his intimate knowledge of the territory about Concord, made him drift into the profession of land-surveyor. It had the advantage for him that it led him continually into new and secluded grounds, and helped his studies of Nature. His accuracy and skill in this work were readily appreciated, and he found all the employment he wanted.

He could easily solve the problems of the surveyor, but he was daily beset with graver questions, which he manfully confronted. He interrogated every custom, and wished to settle all his practice on an ideal foundation. He was a protestant *à l'outrance,* and few lives contain so many renunciations. He was bred to no profession; he never married; he lived alone; he never went to church; he never voted; he refused to pay a tax to the State; he ate no flesh, he drank no wine, he never knew the use of tobacco; and, though a naturalist, he used neither trap nor gun.[1] He chose, wisely, no doubt, for himself, to be the bachelor of thought and Nature. He had no talent for wealth, and knew how to be poor without the least hint of squalor or inelegance. Perhaps he fell into his way of living without forecasting it much, but approved it with later wisdom. "I am often reminded," he wrote in his journal, "that, if I had bestowed on me the wealth of Crœsus, my aims must be still the same, and my means essentially the same." He had no temptations to fight against,—no appetites, no passions, no taste for elegant trifles. A fine house, dress, the manners and talk of highly cultivated people were all thrown away on him. He much preferred a good Indian, and considered these refine-

[1 Before the development of adequate field glasses, naturalists commonly shot specimens they wished to identify.—A.B.A.]

ments as impediments to conversation, wishing to meet his companion on the simplest terms. He declined invitations to dinner-parties, because there each was in every one's way, and he could not meet the individuals to any purpose. "They make their pride," he said, "in making their dinner cost much; I make my pride in making my dinner cost little." When asked at table what dish he preferred, he answered, "The nearest." He did not like the taste of wine, and never had a vice in his life. He said,—"I have a faint recollection of pleasure derived from smoking dried lily-stems, before I was a man. I had commonly a supply of these. I have never smoked anything more noxious."

He chose to be rich by making his wants few, and supplying them himself. In his travels, he used the railroad only to get over so much country as was unimportant to the present purpose, walking hundreds of miles, avoiding taverns, buying a lodging in farmers' and fishermen's houses, as cheaper, and more agreeable to him, and because there he could better find the men and the information he wanted.

There was somewhat military in his nature not to be subdued, always manly and able, but rarely tender, as if he did not feel himself except in opposition. He wanted a fallacy to expose, a blunder to pillory, I may say required a little sense of victory, a roll of the drum, to call his powers into full exercise. It cost him nothing to say No; indeed, he found it much easier than to say Yes. It seemed as if his first instinct on hearing a proposition was to controvert it, so impatient was he of the limitations of our daily thought. This habit, of course, is a little chilling to the social affections; and though the companion would in the end acquit him of any malice or untruth, yet it mars conversation. Hence, no equal companion stood in affectionate relations with one so pure and guileless. "I love Henry," said one of his friends, "but I cannot like him; and as for taking his arm, I should as soon think of taking the arm of an elm-tree."

Yet, hermit and stoic as he was, he was really fond of sympathy, and threw himself heartily and childlike into the company of young people whom he loved, and whom he delighted

124

to entertain, as he only could, with the varied and endless anecdotes of his experiences by field and river. And he was always
ready to lead a huckleberry party or a search for chestnuts or
grapes. Talking, one day, of a public discourse, Henry remarked,
that whatever succeeded with the audience was bad. I said,
"Who would not like to write something which all can read, like
'Robinson Crusoe'? and who does not see with regret that his
page is not solid with a right materialistic treatment, which
delights everybody?" Henry objected, of course, and vaunted
the better lectures which reached only a few persons. But, at
supper, a young girl, understanding that he was to lecture at
the Lyceum, sharply asked him, "whether his lecture would be
a nice, interesting story, such as she wished to hear, or whether
it was one of those old philosophical things that she did not
care about." Henry turned to her, and bethought himself, and,
I saw, was trying to believe that he had matter that might fit
her and her brother, who were to sit up and go to the lecture,
if it was a good one for them.

He was a speaker and actor of the truth,—born such,—and
was ever running into dramatic situations from this cause. In
any circumstance, it interested all bystanders to know what part
Henry would take, and what he would say; and he did not dis-
appoint expectation, but used an original judgment on each
emergency. In 1845 he built himself a small framed house on
the shores of Walden Pond, and lived there two years alone,
a life of labor and study. This action was quite native and fit for
him. No one who knew him would tax him with affection. He
was more unlike his neighbors in his thought than in his action.
As soon as he had exhausted the advantages of that solitude,
he abandoned it. In 1847, not approving some uses to which the
public expenditure was applied, he refused to pay his town
tax, and was put in jail. A friend paid the tax for him,[2] and he
was released. The like annoyance was threatened the next year.
But, as his friends paid the tax, notwithstanding his protest, I
believe he ceased to resist. No opposition or ridicule had any

[2 The friend was Emerson, and the tax $1.—A.B.A.]

weight with him. He coldly and fully stated his opinion of the company. It was of no consequence, if every one present held the opposite opinion. On one occasion he went to the University Library to procure some books. The librarian refused to lend them. Mr. Thoreau repaired to the President, who stated to him the rules and usages, which permitted the loan of books to resident graduates, to clergymen who were alumni, and to some others resident within a circle of ten miles' radius from the College. Mr. Thoreau explained to the President that the railroad had destroyed the old scale of distances,—that the library was useless, yes, and President and College useless, on the terms of his rules,—that the one benefit he owed to the College was its library,—that, at this moment, not only his want of books was imperative, but he wanted a large number of books, and assured him that he, Thoreau, and not the librarian, was the proper custodian of these. In short, the President found the petitioner so formidable, and the rules getting to look so ridiculous, that he ended by giving him a privilege which in his hands proved unlimited thereafter.

No truer American existed than Thoreau. His preference of his country and condition was genuine, and his aversation from English and European manners and tastes almost reached contempt. He listened impatiently to news or *bon mots* gleaned from London circles; and though he tried to be civil, these anecdotes fatigued him. The men were all imitating each other, and on a small mould. Why can they not live as far apart as possible, and each be a man by himself? What he sought was the most energetic nature; and he wished to go to Oregon, not to London. "In every part of Great Britain," he wrote in his diary, "are discovered traces of the Romans, their funereal urns, their camps, their roads, their dwellings. But New England, at least, is not based on any Roman ruins. We have not to lay the foundations of our houses on the ashes of a former civilization."

But, idealist as he was, standing for abolition of slavery, abolition of tariffs, almost for abolition of government, it is needless to say he found himself not only unrepresented in actual politics, but almost equally opposed to every class of reformers. Yet he paid the tribute of his uniform respect to the Anti-Slavery Party. One man, whose personal acquaintance he had formed, he honored with exceptional regard. Before the first friendly word had been spoken for Captain John Brown, after the arrest, he sent notices to most houses in Concord, that he would speak in a public hall on the condition and character of John Brown, on Sunday evening, and invited all people to come. The Republican Committee, the Abolitionist Committee, sent him word that it was premature and not advisable. He replied,—"I did not send to you for advice, but to announce that I am to speak." The hall was filled at an early hour by people of all parties, and his earnest eulogy of the hero was heard by all respectfully, by many with a sympathy that surprised themselves.

It was said of Plotinus that he was ashamed of his body, and 't is very likely he had good reason for it,—that his body was a bad servant, and he had not skill in dealing with the material world, as happens often to men of abstract intellect. But Mr. Thoreau was equipped with a most adapted and serviceable body. He was of short stature, firmly built, of light complexion, with strong, serious blue eyes, and a grave aspect,—his face covered in the late years with a becoming beard. His senses were acute, his frame well-knit and hardy, his hands strong and skillful in the use of tools. And there was a wonderful fitness of body and mind. He could pace sixteen rods more accurately than another man could measure them with rod and chain. He could find his path in the woods at night, he said, better by his feet than his eyes. He could estimate the measure of a tree very well by his eyes; he could estimate the weight of a calf or a pig, like a dealer. From a box containing a bushel or more of loose pencils, he could take up with his hands fast enough just a dozen pencils at every grasp. He was a good swimmer, runner, skater, boatman, and would probably outwalk most countrymen in a day's journey. And the relation of body to mind was still finer than we have indicated. He said he wanted every stride his legs made. The length of his walk uniformly made the length of his writing. If shut up in the house, he did not write at all.

He had a strong common sense, like that which Rose Flammock, the weaver's daughter, in Scott's romance, commends in her father, as resembling a yardstick which, whilst it measures dowlas and diaper, can equally well measure tapestry and cloth of gold. He had always a new resource. When I was planting forest-trees, and had procured half a peck of acorns, he said that only a small portion of them would be sound, and proceeded to examine them, and select the sound ones. But finding this took time, he said, "I think, if you put them all into water, the good ones will sink;" which experiment we tried with success. He could plan a garden, or a house, or a barn; would have been competent to lead a "Pacific Exploring Expedition;" could give judicious counsel in the gravest private or public affairs.

He lived for the day, not cumbered and mortified by his memory. If he brought you yesterday a new proposition, he would bring you to-day another not less revolutionary. A very industrious man, and setting, like all highly organized men, a high value on his time, he seemed the only man of leisure in town, always ready for any excursion that promised well, or for conversation prolonged into late hours. His trenchant sense was never stopped by his rules of daily prudence, but was always up to the new occasion. He liked and used the simplest food, yet, when one urged a vegetable diet, Thoreau thought all diets a very small matter, saying that "the man who shoots the buffalo lives better than the man who boards at the Graham House." He said,—"You can sleep near the railroad, and never be disturbed: Nature knows very well what sounds are worth attending to, and has made up her mind not to hear the railroad-whistle. But things respect the devout mind, and a mental ecstasy was never interrupted." He noted what repeatedly befell him, that, after receiving from a distance a rare plant, he would presently find the same in his own haunts. And those pieces of luck which happen only to good players happened to him. One day, walking with a stranger, who inquired where Indian arrow-heads could be found, he replied, "Everywhere," and, stooping forward, picked one on the instant from the ground. At Mount Washington, in Tuckerman's Ravine, Thoreau had a bad fall, and sprained his foot. As he was in the act of getting up from his fall, he saw for the first time the leaves of the *Arnica mollis*.[3]

His robust common sense, armed with stout hands, keen perceptions, and strong will, cannot yet account for the superiority which shone in his simple and hidden life. I must add the cardinal fact, that there was an excellent wisdom in him, proper to a rare class of men, which showed him the material world as a means and symbol. This discovery, which sometimes yields to poets a certain casual and interrupted light, serving for the ornament of their writing, was in him an unsleeping insight; and whatever faults or obstructions of temperament might cloud it, he was not disobedient to the heavenly vision. In his youth, he said, one day, "The other world is all my art: my pencils will draw no other; my jack-knife will cut nothing else; I do not use it as a means." This was the muse and genius that ruled his opinions, conversation, studies, work and course of life. This made him a searching judge of men. At first glance he measured his companion, and, though insensible to some fine traits of culture, could very well report his weight and calibre. And this made the impression of genius which his conversation often gave.

He understood the matter in hand at a glance, and saw the limitations and poverty of those he talked with, so that nothing seemed concealed from such terrible eyes. I have repeatedly known young men of sensibility converted in a moment to the belief that this was the man they were in search of, the man of men, who could tell them all they should do. His own dealing with them was never affectionate, but superior, didactic, —scorning their petty ways,—very slowly conceding, or not

[3 A yellow, daisy-like flower found in New England only on mountain slopes.— A.B.A.]

conceding at all, the promise of his society at their houses, or
even at his own. "Would he not walk with them?" "He did not
know. There was nothing so important to him as his walk; he
had no walks to throw away on company." Visits were offered
him from respectful parties, but he declined them. Admiring
friends offered to carry him at their own cost to the Yellow-Stone
River,—to the West Indies,—to South America. But though
nothing could be more grave or considered than his refusals,
they remind one in quite new relations of that fop Brummel's
reply to the gentleman who offered him his carriage in a
shower, "But where will *you* ride, then?"—and what accusing
silences, and what searching and irresistible speeches, battering
down all defenses, his companions can remember!

Mr. Thoreau dedicated his genius with such entire love
to the fields, hills, and waters of his native town, that he made
them known and interesting to all reading Americans, and to
people over the sea. The river on whose banks he was born
and died he knew from its springs to its confluence with the
Merrimack. He had made summer and winter observations on
it for many years, and at every hour of the day and night. The
result of the recent survey of the Water Commissioners appointed by the State of Massachusetts he had reached, by his
private experiments, several years earlier. Every fact which
occurs in the bed, on the banks, or in the air over it; the fishes,
and their spawning and nests, their manners, their food; the
shad-flies which fill the air on a certain evening once a year,
and which are snapped at by the fishes so ravenously that many
of these die of repletion; the conical heaps of small stones on
the river-shallows, one of which heaps will sometimes overfill
a cart,—these heaps the huge nests of small fishes; the birds
which frequent the stream, heron, duck, sheldrake, loon, osprey;
the snake, musk-rat, otter, woodchuck, and fox, on the banks;
the turtle, frog, hyla, and cricket, which make the banks vocal,
—were all known to him, and, as it were, townsmen and fellow-
creatures; so that he felt an absurdity or violence in any narrative of one of these by itself apart, and still more of its dimensions

on an inch-rule, or in the exhibition of its skeleton, or the specimen of a squirrel or a bird in brandy. He liked to speak of the manners of the river, as itself a lawful creature, yet with exactness, and always to an observed fact. As he knew the river, so the ponds in this region.

One of the weapons he used, more important than microscope or alcohol-receiver to other investigators, was a whim which grew on him by indulgence, yet appeared in gravest statement, namely, of extolling his own town and neighborhood as the most favored centre for natural observation. He remarked that the Flora of Massachusetts embraced almost all the important plants of America,—most of the oaks, most of the willows, the best pines, the ash, the maple, the beech, the nuts. He returned Kane's "Arctic Voyage" to a friend of whom he had borrowed it, with the remark, that "most of the phenomena noted might be observed in Concord." He seemed a little envious of the Pole, for the coincident sunrise and sunset, or five minutes' day after six months: a splendid fact, which Annursnuc had never afforded him. He found red snow in one of his walks, and told me that he expected to find yet the *Victoria regia* in Concord. He was the attorney of the indigenous plants, and owned to a preference of the weeds to the imported plants, as of the Indian to the civilized man,—and noticed, with pleasure, that the willow bean-poles of his neighbor had grown more than his beans. "See these weeds," he said, "which have been hoed at by a million farmers all spring and summer, and yet have prevailed, and just now come out triumphant over all lanes, pastures, fields, and gardens, such is their vigor. We have insulted them with low names, too,—as Pigweed, Wormwood, Chickweed, Shad-Blossom." He says, "They have brave names, too, —Ambrosia, Stellaria, Amelanchia, Amaranth, etc."

I think his fancy for referring everything to the meridian of Concord did not grow out of any ignorance or depreciation of other longitudes or latitudes, but was rather a playful expression of his conviction of the indifference of all places, and that the best place for each is where he stands. He expressed it once in this wise:—"I think nothing is to be hoped from you, if this bit of mould under your feet is not sweeter to you to eat than any other in this world, or in any world."

The other weapon with which he conquered all obstacles in science was patience. He knew how to sit immovable, a part of the rock he rested on, until the bird, the reptile, the fish, which had retired from him, should come back, and resume its habits, nay, moved by curiosity, should come to him and watch him.

It was a pleasure and a privilege to walk with him. He knew the country like a fox or a bird, and passed through it as freely by paths of his own. He knew every track in the snow or on the ground, and what creature had taken this path before him. One must submit abjectly to such a guide, and the reward was great. Under his arm he carried an old music-book to press plants; in his pocket, his diary and pencil, a spy-glass for birds, microscope, jack-knife, and twine. He wore straw hat, stout shoes, strong gray trousers to brave shrub-oaks and smilax, and to climb a tree for a hawk's or a squirrel's nest. He waded into the pool for the water-plants, and his strong legs were no insignificant part of his armor. On the day I speak of he looked for the Menyanthes, detected it across the wide pool, and, on examination of the florets, decided that it had been in flower five days. He drew out of his breast-pocket his diary, and read the names of all the plants that should bloom on this day, whereof he kept account as a banker when his notes fall due. The Cypripedium not due till to-morrow. He thought, that, if waked up from a trance, in this swamp, he could tell by the plants what time of the year it was within two days. The redstart was flying about, and presently the fine grosbeaks, whose brilliant scarlet makes the rash gazer wipe his eye, and whose fine clear note Thoreau compared to that of a tanager which has got rid of its hoarseness. Presently he heard a note which he called that of the night-warbler, a bird he had never identified, had been in search of twelve years, which always, when he saw it, was in the act of diving down into a tree or bush, and which it was vain to seek; the only bird that sings indifferently by night and by day. I told him he must beware of finding and booking it, lest life should have nothing more to show him. He said, "What you seek in vain for, half your life, one day you come full upon all the family at dinner. You seek it like a dream, and as soon as you find it you become its prey."

His interest in the flower or the bird lay very deep in his mind, was connected with Nature,—and the meaning of Nature was never attempted to be defined by him. He would not offer a memoir of his observations to the Natural History Society. "Why should I? To detach the description from its connections in my mind would make it no longer true or valuable to me; and they do not wish what belongs to it." His power of observation seemed to indicate additional senses. He saw as with microscope, heard as with ear-trumpet, and his memory was a photographic register of all he saw and heard. And yet none knew better than he that it is not the fact that imports, but the impression or effect of the fact on your mind. Every fact lay in glory in his mind, a type of the order and beauty of the whole.

His determination on Natural History was organic. He confessed that he sometimes felt like a hound or a panther, and, if born among Indians, would have been a fell hunter. But, restrained by his Massachusetts culture, he played out the game in this mild form of botany and ichthyology. His intimacy with animals suggested what Thomas Fuller records of Butler the apiologist, that "either he had told the bees things or the bees had told him." Snakes coiled round his leg, the fishes swam into his hand, and he took them out of the water; he pulled the wood-chuck out of its hole by the tail, and took the foxes under his protection from the hunters. Our naturalist had perfect magnanimity; he had no secrets: he would carry you to the heron's haunt, or even to his most prized botanical swamp,—possibly knowing that you could never find it again, yet willing to take his risks.

No college ever offered him a diploma, or a professor's chair; no academy made him its corresponding secretary, its discoverer,

133

or even its member. Perhaps these learned bodies feared the satire of his presence. Yet so much knowledge of Nature's secret and genius few others possessed, none in a more large and religious synthesis. For not a particle of respect had he to the opinions of any man or body of men, but homage solely to the truth itself; and as he discovered everywhere among doctors some leaning of courtesy, it discredited them. He grew to be revered and admired by his townsmen, who had at first known him only as an oddity. The farmers who employed him as a surveyor soon discovered his rare accuracy and skill, his knowledge of their lands, of trees, of birds, of Indian remains, and the like, which enabled him to tell every farmer more than he knew before of his own farm; so that he began to feel as if Mr. Thoreau had better rights in his land than he. They felt, too, the superiority of character which addressed all men with a native authority.

Indian relics abound in Concord,—arrow-heads, stone chisels, pestles, and fragments of pottery; and on the river-bank, large heaps of clam-shells and ashes mark spots which the savages frequented. These, and every circumstance touching the Indian, were important in his eyes. His visits to Maine were chiefly for love of the Indian. He had the satisfaction of seeing the manufacture of the bark-canoe, as well as of trying his hand in its management on the rapids. He was inquisitive about the making of the stone arrow-head, and in his last days charged a youth setting out for the Rocky Mountains to find an Indian who could tell him that: "It was well worth a visit to California to learn it." Occasionally, a small party of Penobscot Indians would visit Concord, and pitch their tents for a few weeks in summer on the river-bank. He failed not to make acquaintance with the best of them; though he well knew that asking questions of Indians is like catechizing beavers and rabbits. In his last visit to Maine he had great satisfaction from Joseph Polis, an intelligent Indian of Oldtown, who was his guide for some weeks.

He was equally interested in every natural fact. The depth of his perception found likeness of law throughout Nature, and

I know not any genius who so swiftly inferred universal law from the single fact. He was no pedant of a department. His eye was open to beauty, and his ear to music. He found these, not in rare conditions, but wheresoever he went. He thought the best of music was in single strains; and he found poetic suggestion in the humming of the telegraph-wire.

His poetry might be bad or good; he no doubt wanted a lyric facility and technical skill; but he had the source of poetry in his spiritual perception. He was a good reader and critic, and his judgment on poetry was to the ground of it. He could not be deceived as to the presence or absence of the poetic element in any composition, and his thirst for this made him negligent and perhaps scornful of superficial graces. He would pass by many delicate rhythms, but he would have detected every live stanza or line in a volume, and knew very well where to find an equal poetic charm in prose. He was so enamored of the spiritual beauty that he held all actual written poems in very light esteem in the comparison. He admired Æschylus and Pindar; but, when some one was commending them, he said that "Æschylus and the Greeks, in describing Apollo and Orpheus, had given no song, or no good one. They ought not to have moved trees, but to have chanted to the gods such a hymn as would have sung all their old ideas out of their heads, and new ones in." His own verses are often rude and defective. The gold does not yet run pure, is drossy and crude. The thyme and marjoram are not yet honey. But if he want lyric fineness and technical merits, if he have not the poetic temperament, he never lacks the causal thought, showing that his genius was better than his talent. He knew the worth of the Imagination for the uplifting and consolation of human life, and liked to throw every thought into a symbol. The fact you tell is of no value, but only the impression. For this reason his presence was poetic, always piqued the curiosity to know more deeply the secrets of his mind. He had many reserves, an unwillingness to exhibit to profane eyes what was still sacred in his own, and knew well how to throw a poetic veil over his experience. All

135

readers of "Walden" will remember his mythical record of his disappointments:—

"I long ago lost a hound, a bay horse, and a turtle-dove, and am still on their trail. Many are the travelers I have spoken [to] concerning them, describing their tracks, and what calls they answered to. I have met one or two who had heard the hound, and the tramp of the horse, and even seen the dove disappear behind a cloud; and they seemed as anxious to recover them as if they had lost them themselves."

His riddles were worth the reading, and I confide, that, if at any time I do not understand the expression, it is yet just. Such was the wealth of his truth that it was not worth his while to use words in vain. His poem entitled "Sympathy" reveals the tenderness under that triple steel of stoicism, and the intellectual subtlety it could animate. His classic poem on "Smoke" suggests Simonides, but is better than any poem of Simonides. His biography is in his verses. His habitual thought makes all his poetry a hymn to the Cause of causes, the Spirit which vivifies and controls his own.

> "I hearing get, who had but ears,
> And sight, who had but eyes before;
> I moments live, who lived but years,
> And truth discern, who knew but learning's lore."

And still more in these religious lines:—

> "Now chiefly is my natal hour,
> And only now my prime of life;
> I will not doubt the love untold,
> Which not my worth or want hath bought,
> Which wooed me young, and wooes me old,
> And to this evening hath me brought."

Whilst he used in his writings a certain petulance of remark in reference to churches or churchmen, he was a person of a rare, tender, and absolute religion, a person incapable of any profanation, by act or by thought. Of course, the same isolation which belonged to his original thinking and living detached him from the social religious forms. This is neither to be censured nor

136

regretted. Aristotle long ago explained it, when he said, "One who surpasses his fellow-citizens in virtue is no longer a part of the city. Their law is not for him, since he is a law to himself."

Thoreau was sincerity itself, and might fortify the convictions of prophets in the ethical laws by his holy living. It was an affirmative experience which refused to be set aside. A truth-speaker he, capable of the most deep and strict conversation; a physician to the wounds of any soul; a friend, knowing not only the secret of friendship, but almost worshipped by those few persons who resorted to him as their confessor and prophet, and knew the deep value of his mind and great heart. He thought that without religion or devotion of some kind nothing great was ever accomplished: and he thought that the bigoted sectarian had better bear this in mind.

His virtues, of course, sometimes ran into extremes. It was easy to trace to the inexorable demand on all for exact truth that austerity which made this willing hermit more solitary even than he wished. Himself of a perfect probity, he required not less of others. He had a disgust at crime, and no worldly success could cover it. He detected paltering as readily in dignified and prosperous persons as in beggars, and with equal scorn. Such dangerous frankness was in his dealing that his admirers called him "that terrible Thoreau," as if he spoke when silent, and was still present when he had departed. I think the severity of his ideal interfered to deprive him of a healthy sufficiency of human society.

The habit of a realist to find things the reverse of their appearance inclined him to put every statement in a paradox. A certain habit of antagonism defaced his earlier writings,—a trick of rhetoric not quite outgrown in his later, of substituting for the obvious word and thought its diametrical opposite. He praised wild mountains and winter forests for their domestic air, in snow and ice he would find sultriness, and commended the wilderness for resembling Rome and Paris. "It was so dry, that you might call it wet."

The tendency to magnify the moment, to read all the laws

of Nature in the one object or one combination under your eye, is of course comic to those who do not share the philosopher's perception of identity. To him there was no such thing as size. The pond was a small ocean; the Atlantic, a large Walden Pond. He referred every minute fact to cosmical laws. Though he meant to be just, he seemed haunted by a certain chronic assumption that the science of the day pretended completeness, and he had just found out that the *savans* had neglected to discriminate a particular botanical variety, had failed to describe the seeds or count the sepals. "That is to say," we replied, "the blockheads were not born in Concord; but who said they were? It was their unspeakable misfortune to be born in London, or Paris, or Rome; but, poor fellows, they did what they could, considering that they never saw Bateman's Pond, or Nine-Acre Corner, or Becky-Stow's Swamp. Besides, what were you sent into the world for, but to add this observation?"

Had his genius been only contemplative, he had been fitted to his life, but with his energy and practical ability he seemed born for great enterprise and for command; and I so much regret the loss of his rare powers of action, that I cannot help counting it a fault in him that he had no ambition. Wanting this, instead of engineering for all America, he was the captain of a huckleberry party. Pounding beans is good to the end of pounding empires one of these days; but if, at the end of years, it is still only beans!

But these foibles, real or apparent, were fast vanishing in the incessant growth of a spirit so robust and wise, and which effaced its defeats with new triumphs. His study of Nature was a perpetual ornament to him, and inspired his friends with curiosity to see the world through his eyes, and to hear his adventures. They possessed every kind of interest.

He had many elegances of his own, whilst he scoffed at conventional elegance. Thus, he could not bear to hear the sound of his own steps, the grit of gravel; and therefore never willingly walked in the road, but in the grass, on mountains and in woods. His senses were acute, and he remarked that by night every dwelling-house gives out bad air, like a slaughter-house. He liked the pure fragrance of melilot. He honored certain plants with special regard, and, over all, the pond-lily,— then, the gentian, and the *Mikania scandens*, and "life-everlast-ing," and a bass-tree which he visited every year when it bloomed, in the middle of July. He thought the scent a more oracular inquisition than the sight,—more oracular and trust-worthy. The scent, of course, reveals what is concealed from the other senses. By it he detected earthiness. He delighted in echoes, and said they were almost the only kind of kindred voices that he heard. He loved Nature so well, was so happy in her solitude, that he became very jealous of cities, and the sad work which their refinements and artifices made with man and his dwelling. The axe was always destroying his forest.

"Thank God," he said, "they cannot cut down the clouds!" "All kinds of figures are drawn on the blue ground with this fibrous white paint."

I subjoin a few sentences taken from his unpublished manu-scripts, not only as records of his thought and feeling, but for their power of description and literary excellence.

"Some circumstantial evidence is very strong, as when you find a trout in the milk."

"The chub is a soft fish, and tastes like boiled brown paper salted."

"The youth gets together his materials to build a bridge to the moon, or, perchance, a palace or temple on the earth, and at length the middle-aged man concludes to build a wood-shed with them."

"The locust z-ing."

"Devil's-needles zigzagging along the Nut-Meadow brook."

"Sugar is not so sweet to the palate as sound to the healthy ear."

"I put on some hemlock-boughs, and the rich salt crackling of their leaves was like mustard to the ear, the crackling of un-countable regiments. Dead trees love the fire."

"The bluebird carries the sky on his back."

"The tanager flies through the green foliage as if it would ignite the leaves."

"If I wish for a horse-hair for my compass sight, I must go to the stable; but the hair-bird, with her sharp eyes, goes to the road."

"Immortal water, alive ever to the superficies."

"Fire is the most tolerable third party."

"Nature made ferns for pure leaves, to show what she could do in that line."

"No tree has so fair a bole and so handsome an instep as the beech."

"How did these beautiful rainbow-tints get into the shell of the fresh-water clam, buried in the mud at the bottom of our dark river?"

"Hard are the times when the infant's shoes are second-foot."

"We are strictly confined to our men to whom we give liberty."

"Nothing is so much to be feared as fear. Atheism may comparatively be popular with God himself."

"Of what significance the things you can forget? A little thought is sexton to all the world."

"How can we expect a harvest of thought who have not had a seed-time of character?"

"Only he can be trusted with gifts who can present a face of bronze to expectations."

"I ask to be melted. You can only ask of the metals that they be tender to the fire that melts them. To nought else can they be tender."

There is a flower known to botanists, one of the same genus with our summer plant called "life-everlasting," a *Gnaphalium* like that which grows on the most inaccessible cliffs of the Tyrolese mountains, where the chamois dare hardly venture, and which the hunter, tempted by its beauty, and by his love, (for it is immensely valued by the Swiss maidens), climbs the cliffs to gather, and is sometimes found dead at the foot, with the flower in his hand. It is called by botanists the *Gnaphalium leontopodium,* but by the Swiss *Edelweiss,* which signifies *Noble*

Purity. Thoreau seemed to me living in the hope to gather this plant, which belonged to him of right. The scale on which his studies proceeded was so large as to require longevity, and we were the less prepared for his sudden disappearance. The country knows not yet, or in the least part, how great a son it has lost. It seems an injury that he should leave in the midst his broken task, which none else can finish,—a kind of indignity to so noble a soul, that it should depart out of Nature before yet he has been really shown to his peers for what he is. But he, at least, is content. His soul was made for the noblest society; he had in a short life exhausted the capabilities of this world; wherever there is knowledge, wherever there is virtue, wherever there is beauty, he will find a home.

Index

Index

144

Where to Stop

When Thoreau made a journey, he preferred to go by foot and looked only for the simplest of food and lodging. But today's traveler—both by circumstance and by nature—is not so casual in his arrangements and therefore may find the following list helpful. The names have been drawn from two authorities, The American Automobile Association and Duncan Hines, who have each issued directories containing more detailed information.

BASS RIVER

BASS RIVER MOTEL—State 28, 3¾ mi. e. of Hyannis. Swimming pool.

BLUE WATER MOTEL—South Shore Dr., 1 mi. s. of State 28. Oceanfront. Private beach. Swimming pool. No children under 10.

CORRAL MOTEL—State 28, 4 mi. e. of Hyannis. Swimming Pool.

OCEAN MIST MOTOR LODGE—South Shore Dr., 1 mi. s. of State 28. Oceanfront. Private beach. No children under 9.

NEW CAVALIER—3 mi. s. of Hyannis. Swimming pool. Recreation room.

RIVIERA MOTEL—South Shore Dr., 1 mi. s. of State 28. Oceanfront. Swimming pool.

SEA VIEW MOTEL—Seaview Ave., 3 mi. e. of Hyannis. 2 swimming pools.

THE SURFCOMBER—South Shore Dr., 1 mi. s. of State 28. Oceanfront. Private beach. Swimming pool. No children under 8.

SURF & SAND MOTEL—South Shore Dr., 1 mi. s. of State 28. Private beach.

VILLAGE GREEN MOTEL—South Shore Dr., 1 mi. s. of State 28. Swimming pool. Recreations room. *Breakfast*. No children under 6.

BREWSTER

SKYLINE MOTEL—State 6A., 1 mi. w. of town.

BUZZARD'S BAY

AUSTRIA MOTEL—U.S. 6 & State 28, 3 mi. w. of town.

BURT'S MOTEL—State 28, 2 mi. s.e. of town.

BUZZARD'S BAY MOTOR LODGE—U.S. 6 & State 28, ¾ mi. w. of town. On bay. Private beach. Fishing & boat dock.

PANORAMA MOTOR LODGE—At traffic circle, 2 mi. s.e. of town. Overlooks canal. *Coffee shop & cocktail lounge*.

REDWOOD MOTEL—U.S. 6 & State 28, 1 mi. e. of town. Swimming pool.

WOODCHIPS MOTOR INN—U.S. 6 & State 28, 3½ mi. w. of town. Swimming pool. *Cocktail lounge. Breakfast & dinner*.

CENTERVILLE

CORAL VILLAGE—On Craigville beach. Cottages. Fireplaces. Rowboats.

CRAIG VILLAGE BY-THE-SEA—On Craigville beach. Cottages. Fireplaces.

CRAIGVILLE MOTEL—U.S. 6 & State 132. Swimming pool.

TRADE WINDS INN & CLUB—On Craigville Beach. *Breakfast & dinner. Cocktail lounge*.

CHATHAM

DAUPHIN COURT MOTEL—362 Main St. Rooms & 1 cottage.

EBB TIDE MOTEL—State 28, 1¼ mi. w. of town. Overlooks Oyster Pond. Swimming pool. Lawn games. *Breakfast*.

HAWTHORNE MOTEL—Shore Rd., 1 mi. n. of town. On bay. Private beach.

PLEASANT BAY VILLAGE—State 28, 1 mi. n. of town. Cottages and apts. Swimming pool. Lawn games.

RELIANCE MOTEL—State 28, 3¼ mi. w. of town. Lawn games.

CHRISTOPHER RYDER HOUSE—State 28, 3 mi. n. of town. No rooms. *Restaurant. Cocktail lounge. Dinner* 6 P.M.-10 P.M. Dancing to 1 A.M.

WAYSIDE INN—Main St. Old stagecoach inn. Rooms and *meals*.

COTUIT

MERRY MEADOWS MOTEL—Falmouth Rd., 1 mi. n.e. of town. Private beach. Lounge. Sun deck. *Breakfast.*

DENNIS PORT

BEACH FRONT APTS.—Old Wharf Rd., 1½ mi. s.e. of jct. State 28 & 134. Private beach. No children under 8.

CAPE PINE MOTEL—1¾ mi. s.e. of State jct. 28 & 134. *Coffee shop. Cocktail lounge.*

COLONY BEACH MOTEL—Old Wharf Rd., 1¼ mi. s. of State 28. Oceanfront. Swimming pool. Private beach. No children under 10.

GASLIGHT RESORT MOTEL—Chase Ave., 1¼ mi. s. via Belmont Rd.

LAMPLIGHTER MOTOR LODGE—State 28, ½ mi. w. of town. Swimming pool.

LAUDERDALE RESORT MOTEL—Capt. Chase Rd., 2½ mi. s.e. of State 28 & 134. Children only by special arrangement.

NEW SPOUTER WHALE MOTOR INN—Old Wharf Rd., 1¼ mi. s. of State 28. Oceanfront. Private beach. *Breakfast.*

SHIFTING SANDS MOTEL—Chase Ave., 1¼ mi. s. of State 28. Oceanfront. Private beach.

SOUNDINGS RESORT MOTEL—Chase Ave., 1¼ mi. s. of State 28. Oceanfront. Swimming pool. Private beach. No children under 10.

WILLIAM & MARY MOTEL—Lower County Rd., 1 mi. s. of town. Swimming pool. Recreation room.

EAST BREWSTER

CHILLINGWORTH—State 6A, 1½ mi. w. of town. No rooms. *Restaurant. Cocktail lounge.* Open 6 A.M.-10 P.M. (Clsd. Mon.)

EASTHAM

CRANBERRY COTTAGES—U.S. 6, 2 mi. s. of town.

EAGLE WING MOTEL—U.S. 6, 1¾ mi. s. of town.

ROUTE 6 MOTEL—U.S. 6, 1½ mi. n. of town. *Breakfast.*

SALT POND MOTEL—U.S. 6, ¼ mi. n. of town. Private beach. *Breakfast.*

FALMOUTH

COONAMESSETT INN—Jones Rd. & Gifford St., ½ mi. n. of State 28. Rooms. *Restaurant* open 8 A.M.-10 A.M.; noon-3 P.M.; 6 P.M.-9 P.M. *Cocktail lounge.*

FALMOUTH HEIGHTS MOTOR LODGE—146 Falmouth Heights Rd. On harbor.

FLYING BRIDGE RESTAURANT—Scranton Ave. on Falmouth Harbor. *Indoor and outdoor dining. Cocktail lounge.* Open 5 P.M.-10:30 P.M.

GENERAL SWIFT MOTEL—824 E. Main St. Swimming pool. Recreation bldg.

MARINER MOTOR INN—Main St. Rooms. *Restaurant.* Playground.

STUDIO MOTEL—Falmouth Heights Rd. On harbor.

VAN DYKE MOTEL—State 28, 7 mi. e. of town. Swimming pool.

HARWICHPORT

LINCOLN LODGE & MARY TODD COURT—Lower County Rd., 1 block s. of State 28. Rooms. Cottages. *Restaurant.* Lawn games. Bathhouse.

STONE HORSE MOTEL—State 28, 1½ mi. e. of town.

TROY COURT—28 Sea St., ¼ mi. s. of State 28.

HYANNIS

AMERICAN HOLIDAY MOTEL—State 28, 1 mi. e. of town. Swimming pool.

ANGEL MOTEL—State 132, 1¼ mi. n.w. of town. Swimming pool.

BELLE INGRAM MOTEL—Centerville Rd., 1½ mi. w. via Main St.

BRADFORD MOTEL—State 28, ½ mi. w. of State 132 jct. *Breakfast.*

CANDLELIGHT MOTOR LODGE—447 Main St.

CAPT. GOSNOLD VILLAGE—Gosnold St., 1 mi. s. via Sea St.

COUNTRY LAKE MOTEL—State 132, 3¼ mi. n.w. of town. Lakefront. Private beach. Swimming pool. Rowboats. Fishing. Lawn games.

GORDON FRANCIS MOTEL—State 28, 1.4 mi. w. jct. State 132. On pond. *Breakfast.*

HYANNIS INN MOTEL—473 Main St. *Breakfast & lunch. Cocktail lounge.* Swimming pool.

HYANNIS STAR MOTEL—State 132, 2 mi. n.w. of town. *Breakfast & lunch.* Swimming pool.

JAMES STEPHENS MOTEL—State 28, 1 mi. e. jct. State 132. Swimming pool.

LAMPLIGHTER MOTEL—State 132, 1¼ mi. n.w. of town. Swimming pool. Tennis.

MUNN'S MOTEL—State 132, 2¼ mi. n.w. of town. Swimming pool.

PORT 'N STARBOARD MOTEL—State 132, 2¼ mi. n.w. of town. Swimming pool.

RAINBOW MOTEL—State 132, 3 mi. n.w. of town. On lake. Private beach. Swimming pool. Boats. Fishing. *Breakfast & lunch.*

RED COACH GRILL—Jct. State 28 & 132, 1 mi. n. of town. *Restaurant. Cocktail lounge.* Open 4 P.M.-11 P.M. Sun. noon—3 P.M.

NEPTUNE ROOM—Jct. State 28 & 132, 1 mi. n. of town, in Municipal Airport Bldg. *Restaurant.* Open 4 P.M.-midnight. Sun. 11:30 A.M.-midnight. *Cocktail lounge.*

TOP O' THE MORN MOTOR LODGE—State 132, 2½ mi. n.w. of town. Swimming pool.

WINDRIFT MOTEL—State 28, 1 mi. e. of town. Swimming pool.

YACHTSMAN—Ocean St., 1 mi. s. of town. On bay. Rooms & cottages. *Restaurant. Cocktail lounge. Beach bar.* Private beach. Swimming pool. Steam baths. Lawn games. Boat dock. *Clambakes.*

HYANNISPORT

HARBOR VILLAGE—Marstons Ave., off Ocean Ave. & Sea St. Across from ocean. Fireplaces. Boats.

NORTH EASTHAM

NEW VOYAGER MOTEL INN—Mid-Cape Hwy., 3½ mi. n. of town. *Restaurant.* Lounge. Sundeck. Playground. Swimming pool.

NORTH FALMOUTH

COONAMESSETT CORNER—Jct. State 28 & 151. *Restaurant. Cocktail lounge.* Open 5 P.M.-10 P.M.

NORTH TRURO

PETER'S HILL MOTOR LODGE—¼ mi. s. of town. *Restaurant. Cocktail lounge.* Sun deck. Playground. *Clambake* every Thurs. night.

ORLEANS

COVE MOTEL—State 28, ¼ mi. n. of town. On Town Cove. Swimming pool. Rowboats. *Breakfast.*

GOVERNOR PRENCE MOTOR LODGE—Jct. State 6A & 28, ¼ mi. n. of town. *Breakfast & lunch. Cocktail lounge.* Swimming pool.

NAUSET KNOLL MOTOR LODGE—At Nauset Beach, 3 mi. e. via Main St. & Beach Rd. Oceanfront.

OLD TAVERN MOTEL—State 6A, ¼ mi. s.w. of town.

SKAKET BEACH MOTEL—State 6A, ½ mi. s.w. of town. *Breakfast.* Swimming pool.

PROVINCETOWN

BLUE SEA MOTEL—State 6A, 2½ mi. s.e. of town. On bay. Private beach. Swimming pool.

BONNIE DOONE RESTAURANT—State 6A, at 35 Brafford St. *Dining room* open 11 A.M.-11 P.M. *Cocktail lounge* open to 1 A.M.

BRADFORD HOUSE & MOTEL—State 6A, at 41 Bradford St.

CHATEAU MOTEL—State 6A, ¾ mi. w. of town. Rooms & cottages. Fireplaces.

EAST HARBOUR MOTEL & COTTAGES—State 6A, 3 mi. s.e. of town. On bay. Private beach. Fireplaces.

FLAGSHIP RESTAURANT—463 Commercial St. Dining room open noon-midnight. *Cocktail lounge* open to 1 A.M.

GOVERNOR PRENCE MOTOR LODGE—U.S. 6, 4½ mi. s.e. of town. On bay. *Restaurant. Cocktail lounge.* Swimming pool.

KALMAR VILLAGE—State 6A, ¾ mi. s.e. of town. On bay. Private beach.

THE MEADOWS—State 6A, ¾ mi. w. of town. Rooms & cottages. Private beach. Fishing. Guide trips.

PILGRIM COLONY MOTEL—State 6A, 2½ mi. s.e. of town. Rooms & cottages. Fireplaces. Private beach.

PROVINCETOWN INN & MOTEL—1 Commercial St. On bay. *Dining room. Coffee shop. Cocktail lounge.* Swimming pool. Private beach. Boats.

SEA GULL MOTEL—State 6A, 2½ mi. s.e. of town. On bay. Private beach.

SAGAMORE

SHIPS WAY MOTEL—Jct. U.S. 6 & State 3, ¼ mi. s.e. of traffic circle. Rooms & cottages. Overlooks canal. *Breakfast.*

SIERRA MOTEL—Jct. U.S. 6 & State 6A. *Coffee shop.* Swimming pool.

WINDMILL MOTEL—Jct. U.S. 6 & State 6 A. *Coffee shop.* Swimming pool.

SANDWICH

DUNHAM'S MOTOR COURT—State 6A. Faces canal and bay.

OLD COLONY MOTEL—State 6A, 3½ mi. e. of town. Swimming pool.

SHADY NOOK MOTEL—State 6A, 1⅛ mi. w. of town. Rooms & 1 cottage.

THAYER'S COURT—State 6A, ¾ mi. e. of town. Rooms & 1 cottage.

SOUTH YARMOUTH

BEACH 'N TOWNE MOTEL—State 28, ¼ mi. w. of town. Swimming pool. Recreation room.

CAPT. JONATHAN MOTEL—State 28, ¼ mi. w. of town. Rooms & 1 cottage. Swimming pool.

WEST DENNIS

THE PRATCHES MOTEL—State 28, 1 mi. s. of town.

WEST HARWICH

BELMONT HOTEL—Belmont Rd., off State 28, 1 mi. s. of town. Oceanfront. Private beach. *Dining room. 3 cocktail lounges.* Recreation room. Putting greens. Tennis. Lawn games. Children's counselor. Fishing.

THE OLD CHASE HOUSE—State 28. *Restaurant* open 5 P.M.-9 P.M. Sun. noon-9 P.M. *Cocktail lounge.*

WEST YARMOUTH

CAPE TRAVELER MOTEL—State 28, 2 mi. e. of Hyannis. Swimming pool.

HOLIDAY HEARTH MOTELS—State 28, 2 mi. e. of Hyannis. 2 swimming pools.

WOODS HOLE

NAUTILUS MOTOR INN—Main Rd., ¼ mi. n. of town. Overlooks harbor. *Restaurant. Cocktail lounge.* Swimming pool. Putting greens.

SLEEPY HOLLOW MOTEL—Main Rd., ⅓ mi. n. of town. *Breakfast. Coffee bar.* Swimming pool.

YARMOUTH PORT

THE CRANBERRY GOOSE—State 6A, ½ mi. w. of town. *Cottage dining room* open noon-2 P.M.; 5:30 P.M.-8:30 P.M.

OLD YARMOUTH INN—State 6A, center of town. No rooms. *Dining room* open noon-2 P.M.; 5:30 P.M.-9 P.M. *Cocktail lounge.*

THE VILLAGE INN—Main St. Rooms. *Breakfast. Lounge.*

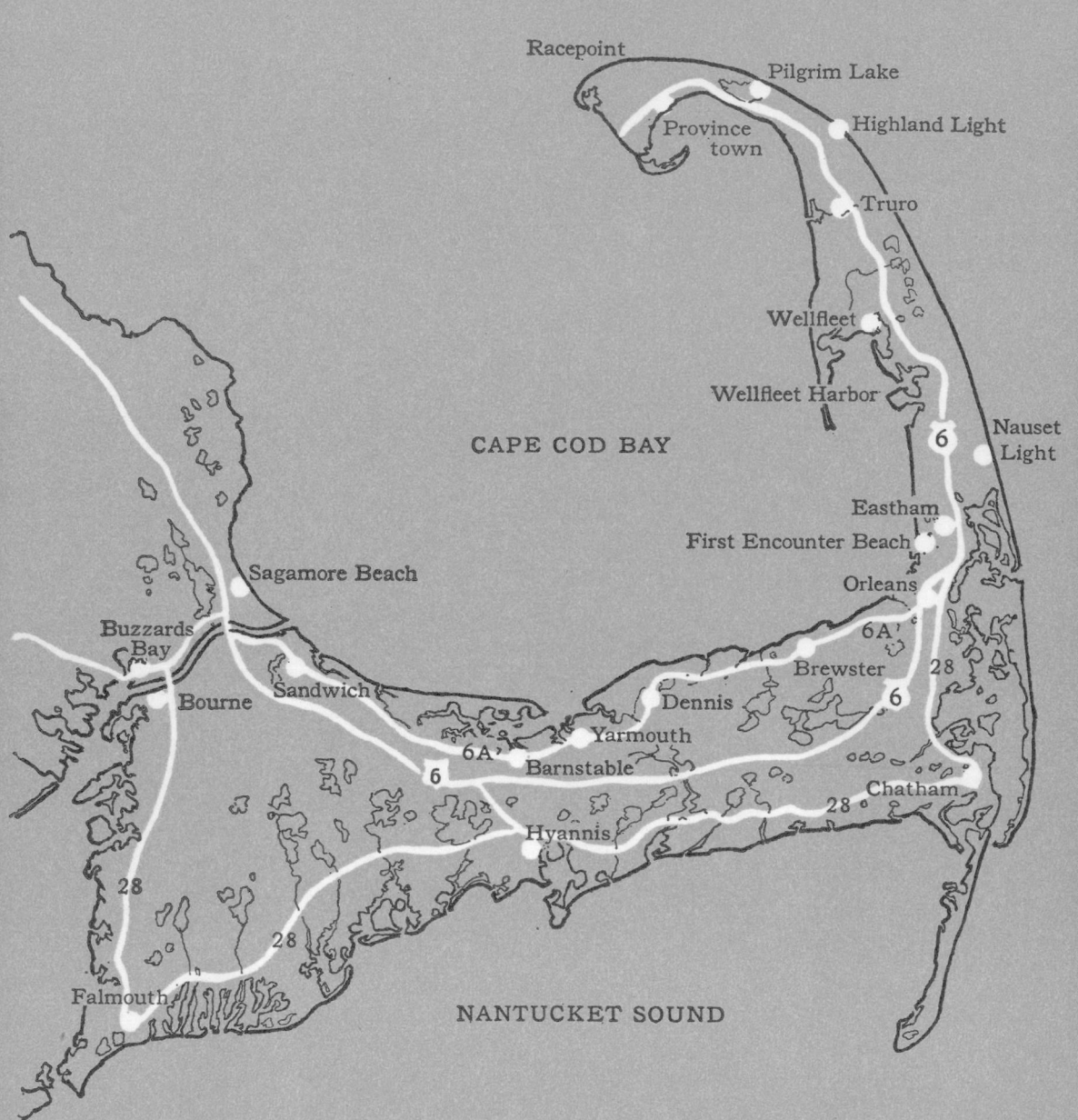

Racepoint

Pilgrim Lake

Province
town

Highland Light

Truro

Wellfleet

Wellfleet Harbor

Nauset
Light

CAPE COD BAY

6

Eastham

First Encounter Beach

Sagamore Beach

Orleans

6A

Buzzards
Bay

Brewster

28

Bourne

Sandwich

6

Dennis

Yarmouth

6A

28

Barnstable

Chatham

6

Falmouth

Hyannis

28

28

NANTUCKET SOUND